Life

After the White House

～ Life ～

After the White House

Press Coverage
of Four Ex-Presidents

Clement E. Asante

PRAEGER

Westport, Connecticut
London

Library of Congress Cataloging-in-Publication Data

Asante, Clement E.
  Life after the White House : press coverage of four ex-Presidents / by Clement E. Asante.
    p. cm.
  Includes bibliographical references and index.
  ISBN 0–275–96266–0 (alk. paper)
    1. Ex-presidents—United States.   2. Ex-presidents—Press coverage—United
States. I. Title.
  JK606.A73   2002
  973.92′092′2—dc21   2001036678

British Library Cataloguing in Publication Data is available.

Library of Congress Catalog Card Number: 2001036678
ISBN: 0–275–96266–0

First published in 2002

Praeger Publishers, 88 Post Road West, Westport, CT 06881
An imprint of Greenwood Publishing Group, Inc.
www.praeger.com

Printed in the United States of America

The paper used in this book complies with the
Permanent Paper Standard issued by the National
Information Standards Organization (Z39.48–1984).

10 9 8 7 6 5 4 3 2 1

Copyright Acknowledgments

The author and publisher gratefully acknowledge permission for use of the following:

"Carter Reminds Reagan of One-China Commitment" by Michael Parks. Copyright, 1981, Los
Angeles Times. Reprinted by permission.

"Mr. Reagan Finally Leads on Guns." Copyright © 1991 by the New York Times Co. Reprinted
by permission.

*To all those who are working diligently to strengthen
the institution of the American presidency.*

Contents

Tables

Acknowledgments

I wish to express my special appreciation to the four former American presidents and elder statesmen—Gerald Ford, Jimmy Carter, Ronald Reagan, and George Bush—who provided the opportunity to enable me to undertake this extraordinary scholarly exercise. Their presidential libraries and websites provided me with ample materials for the study. Similarly, I am indebted to the three leading American newspapers—the *Los Angeles Times*, the *New York Times*, and the *Washington Post*—whose ex-presidential coverage provided to some extent the prism to understanding life after the presidency.

I am extremely grateful to the staff of Greenwood Press, especially Cynthia Harris, Erin Carter, Maureen Melino, and Lindsay Claire, whose patience, advice, and great skills made this book project possible. I also am very appreciative of the invaluable service of Nina Duprey and her extraordinarily able team who saw to the timely production of this book.

Most important, I thank the dedicated staff of the Library of Congress and the Howard University Library System, both in Washington, D.C., for providing the congenial atmosphere and enthusiastic assistance when I was researching materials for this study. Furthermore, I thank Dr. Steven H. Hochman, of the Cater Center in Atlanta, Georgia, for his helpful comments after reading an earlier draft of this manuscript.

I wish to acknowledge the assistance of Joy Egbunike, Ph.D., of Clemson University, in helping to identify some materials and the research instruments used in this study. To Frank Reuter, Ph.D., I express my utmost appreciation for offering useful comments, helpful suggestions, and generally helping to improve the quality of this manuscript.

Finally, I am especially indebted to Betty N. Ezuma, Ph.D., who has been, as always, my unbridled support and continuing source of inspiration in all my research endeavors. Please note that responsibility for contents of this study remains mine, and mine only.

Chapter 1

Introduction

OVERVIEW

In 2000 four former presidents were still alive after serving in the White House for the first time in modern American political history. These ex-presidents were Gerald Rudolph Ford (1974–1977), James Earl Carter Jr. (1977–1981), Ronald Wilson Reagan (1981–1989), and George Herbert Walker Bush (1989–1993) while Bill Clinton still had a few months remaining in office. This study critically and systematically examines how each of these four ex-presidents was treated in the press for three years after leaving the White House. More specifically, it examines the nature and scope of the relationship between the press and the ex-presidents. The study assumes that although they were officially out of office and, thus, out of the political limelight, they, nonetheless, had powerful influence domestically and internationally. Certainly, it would be valuable to know how—and with what intensity, if any—the American press covers these four ex-presidents.

Over the years these ex-presidents have appeared together in several national and international events covered by the media, which told us how they were spending their retirement years. For example, in September 1993, history was made when three out of the five ex-presidents (Richard Milhous Nixon was alive then)—Ford, Carter, and Bush—converged on Washington, D.C., in an unprecedented historic reunion to throw their weight and support behind the North American Free Trade Agreement (NAFTA). The influential support of these elder statesmen played a significant role in swinging the votes toward congressional passage. Then on April 27, 1994, all four former presidents—Ford, Carter, Reagan, and Bush—joined President Bill Clinton in a historic, but solemn, gathering at Yorba Linda, California, honoring the passing of America's 37th president, Richard Nixon. In early November 1995 Carter and Bush joined President Clinton on a high-level U.S. delegation to attend the burial of assassinated Israeli prime minister Yitzhak Rabin. In May 1997 Bush and Ford joined President Clinton to attend the burial in Rabat, Morocco, of King Hassan, who had died of a heart attack. Another ex-presidential reunion for a cause took place on May 9, 2000, at the White House East Room when Ford and Carter joined Clinton at an event to promote America's permanent normal trade relations with the People's Republic of China. The most recent occasion that the ex-presidents came together was on September 14, 2001, during the national day of prayer and remembrance at the Washington National Cathedral following the September 11 terrorists attacks on the World Trade Center in New York and the Pentagon near Washington, D.C. Joining President George W. Bush at this solemn ceremony in the nation's capital were Ford, Carter, Bush (Sr.), and Clinton.

Individually, although they are now out of public office, these ex-presidents continue to dedicate their lives to the service of their country and the outside world, with the exception of Reagan, who now has Alzheimer's disease. For example, Jimmy Carter is known for his antipoverty campaigns, world peace advocacies, and human rights initiatives, particularly in Haiti, Bosnia, Rwanda, Nigeria, the Middle East, and the Korean peninsula; Reagan before his illness for his help in easing the pain of the 1993 earthquake victims in southern California; Bush for his "Thousand Points of Lights" project geared toward volunteerism and scholarship; and Ford for his participation in several conferences and initiatives to bring about peace, harmony, and democracy throughout the world.

RATIONALE FOR THE BOOK

Life After the White House: Press Coverage of Four Ex-Presidents is an attempt to analyze systematically American press coverage of four ex-presidents to learn what kind of press treatment they are getting now that they are private citizens, out of public office. This study is grounded in two propositions: first, that these former leaders continue to make a difference in American social and political lives and, therefore, should receive more attention from the media; and second, that it is very important that the relationship between the press and the ex-presidents be explored to determine its nature and direction. For example, one might anticipate that this relationship will be less adversarial than when they were chief executives with tremendous decision-making and veto powers.

Several studies have shown that the press was not kind to these men while in power. Can we assume that it will now be kind to them because they left the hot seat of the presidency? In truth, we would not know the answer to this important question unless we empirically test this supposition, and this study does just that.

This study is important for three vital reasons. First, since these former U.S. presidents are still under the direct care and protection of the federal government, supported by the American taxpayer, their lives—and particularly the kinds of press coverage or treatment that they get—should concern all Americans. Second, the study hopes to document their post–White House careers through the prism of the press. In doing so, the study can contribute to enriching our understanding of life after the presidency. Third, the study's biographical insights coupled with bibliographical entries can reveal several interesting facts and less-known personality and character traits about these ex-presidents. In short, this study not only depicts the types of press coverage that these elder statesmen are getting but illuminates their lives and works as icons of American political history.

To date, no study empirically examines how the American press covers all the country's former leaders. In short, no one has yet written a book or conducted a study dealing exclusively with the relationship between these ex-presidents and the press. Thus, this study gives us a clear idea of how these four ex-presidents were treated by the newspapers after they left office.

RESEARCH ON THE PRESIDENCY AND THE MEDIA

While in office, these four elder statesmen, like the presidents before them, received intense press criticism and scrutiny. As John Tebbel and Sarah M. Watts note in their comprehensive book *The Press and the Presidency: From George Washington to Ronald Reagan*, published in 1985: "No president has escaped press criticism and no president has considered himself fairly treated" (p. 3). In fact, press coverage of the American presidency continues to be a major area of study in political communication (see Johnston, 1990). Several studies have documented the nature of the relationship between the media and the president, and various assumptions have been made regarding this relationship. For example, in his pioneering book titled *The Presidents and the Press*, James Pollard (1947) looked at relations between the presidents and the press from George Washington to Franklin D. Roosevelt and later with paperback supplements ending with Harry S. Truman.

In his book *President Nixon and the Press*, James Keogh (1972) observes that Nixon came to the presidency not only without the support of most of the men and women who reported the news and commented on it but with their active opposition. He says that Nixon "also came to office determined not to let the attitude of the news media control or even influence his policies—although he well knew that the waves of opinion which they could help to create among the people could affect both his options and his course of action" (p. 7). Eventually, Nixon resigned the presidency in disgrace early in August 1974 in the aftermath of the Watergate scandal.

Mark J. Rozell (1989), in *The Press and the Carter Presidency*, notes that Carter received negative press coverage because he failed to live up to the standards of success that he set for himself and his administration. Said Rozell: "The almost daily press discussions of the president's leadership skills, competence, character and political acumen placed continual demands upon the White House to explain its activities, goals and priorities. The negative press portrait of the president significantly influenced the ability of the White House to carry out its daily activities" (p. 232).

In another study titled *The Press and the Ford Presidency*, Rozell (1992) says that journalists assessed Gerald Ford according to a standard of leadership that he never presumed to achieve. "He played a largely defensive role, using his powers to resist congressional Democrats in their efforts to control the policy agenda. This leadership role clearly did not conform to journalists' notions of presidential activism, and Ford's press image suffered as a result" (p. 232).

In yet another presidential study, Rozell (1996) offers a comprehensive review of press coverage of the Bush presidency. He writes that Bush's openness toward the press did little to improve the nature of his coverage. According to him, "Journalists still characterized the Bush presidency as lacking an agenda and the president himself as lacking 'a vision' for the nation's future" (p. 3).

Ronald Reagan also had his fair share of media criticisms. Carolyn Smith (1990) writes that Reagan was "particularly irritated with reporters who sought out individual examples of hardship and then concluded from single examples that administration economic policy was a failure" (p. 5). Although Reagan used television to his advantage, he occasionally faulted the networks for shedding bad light on his administration. As Michael B. Grossman and Martha J. Kumar (1981) note, "Presidents have tended to blame their inability to achieve desired policy outcomes on the press because of its role in publicizing their administrations' failures" (p. 253).

Other scholars have also conducted insightful studies on president–press relationships, including James Deakin (1984), Robert S. Harper (1951), George Juergens (1981), Frank Lutter Lott (1943), Hoyt Purvis (1976), Richard Rubin (1981), Fredric T. Smoller (1990), M. L. Stein (1969), Rodger Streitmatter (1985), Kenneth W. Thompson (1988), and Graham White (1979). In summing up president–press relations, Smith (1990) argues that "the president and the press are compelled by a conflict of interest to be adversaries." She writes: "The inherent drama is played to conclusion every time there is a direct contact between the two institutions. The adversaries can avoid sustained hostility, but sometimes both parties must pull back to keep the delicate balance intact" (p. 10).

RESEARCH QUESTIONS

The study raised these four research questions:

RQ1   How much press coverage is given to the ex-presidents?

RQ2:   What is the nature of the relationship between the press and the four ex-presidents?

RQ3:   What are the nature and treatment of ex-presidential issues in the American press?

RQ4:   What is the general tone of news items on these four U.S. ex-presidents?

The foregoing questions are answered by analyzing three leading, influential American newspapers, the *Los Angeles Times*, the *New York Times*, and the *Washington Post*. These national newspapers are ranked among the country's most respected and most widely read.

RESEARCH DESIGN AND METHOD

This pioneering study uses content analysis technique to investigate the content and tone of ex-presidential news. Content analysis can help measure the importance that the newspapers attach to ex-presidential news stories by noting the intensity and frequency with which they carry such stories. The study periods are Ford, 1977–1979; Carter, 1981–1983, Reagan, 1989–1991; Bush, 1993–1995. The unit of analysis was the individual stories published about the activities of these ex-presidents from a day after the January 20 presidential inauguration to three years later. Stories concerning their families, friends, associates, and former staff members were excluded.

The ex-presidential stories were content-analyzed or coded as follows:

1. The number of stories was counted to determine the frequency with which these elder statesmen were covered by the selected leading American newspapers.
2. The types of stories (i.e., news story, editorial, feature/commentary, letter to the editor, book review, or cartoon) were counted to establish how ex-presidential news was presented to the public.
3. The emphasis placed on the stories (i.e., front page or inside page) was noted to find out what importance or prominence the press gave to ex-presidential stories.
4. The length of each story was measured by counting the column inches. Each was then identified as long, medium, or short. Here, the predetermined story length designations provided under each newspaper's index were used to identify the length of the story. In the event that the story length was not provided, the story was measured using the *Los Angeles Times* designation style: small was determined by a story up to 6 inches, medium was determined by length of 6 to 18 inches, and long for stories longer than 18 inches. The simple premise was that the longer the story, the more importance that the newspaper attached to it.
5. To determine the major issue of each ex-presidential story, the following eight general categories or subjects were used:
    Awards/honors: References to awards, honors, dinners, birthdays, anniversaries, inaugurations, fund-raising, and so forth.
    Recreation/vacation: Stories dealing with travel, vacations, relocations, social life, amusements, outdoor activities, and so forth.
    Politics: All activities of government as well as stories about political parties, elections, legislation, campaigning, referenda, reforms, endorsements, domestic issues, and international affairs, among others.
    Economy: Stories about finance, federal budget, money, prices, taxes, investment, national debt, inflation, income, labor, salary, natural resources, and so forth.
    Health: References to public and personal health, illness, diagnosis, surgery, mental health, accidents, deaths, funerals, and so forth.

Education: Stories about the country's educational system, students, teachers, lectures, conferences, books, and libraries, as well as school instruction and standards.

Judiciary: Stories dealing with trials, criminal sentences, indictments, investigations, subpoenas, court rulings, grand juries, testimonies, arrests, and so forth.

Other: All stories that do not fit into any of the abovementioned categories with regard to the ex-presidents.

The rationale was to find out how much emphasis the press put on the foregoing categories.

6.   Besides coding each story on the basis of placement, content categories, and length, it was also coded according to its portrayal of the ex-presidents—favorable, neutral, unfavorable. Each paragraph in a story was evaluated and rated as favorable (+), neutral (0), unfavorable (-). For example, a story was classified as favorable if the majority of the paragraphs were positive with regard to their reference to the ex-president in question. Conversely, if the majority of the paragraphs were negative toward the ex-president, the story was classified as unfavorable. In the end the numbers were tabulated, and the tone or direction of the story was determined by the majority of the paragraphs. Stories that vacillated between favorable and unfavorable or that did not have majority direction were coded neutral.

SAMPLING

A systematic sampling of the three American newspapers was drawn for the four ex-presidential periods studied to determine the amount of press coverage given to the ex-presidents. The study periods are Ford—January 21, 1977, to December 31, 1979; Carter—January 21, 1981, to December 31, 1983; Reagan—January 21, 1989, to December 31, 1991; Bush—January 21, 1993, to December 31, 1995. Copies of the three newspapers—*Los Angeles Times*, the *New York Times*, and the *Washington Post*—on microfilm were obtained for analysis. A sample of newspaper stories over time on the ex-presidents was drawn using the index sections of the three newspapers; all stories indexed under the name of each ex-president were identified. Then every fourth story on the list was systematically selected for analysis. If the story did not primarily focus on the ex-president in question, it was dropped from the sample and the next story on the index list was substituted. Also, additional stories identified under other headings in the newspapers' indexes were purposively included in the final sample. For example, other stories were identified under subjects such as Watergate affair, Iran–Contra affair, and presidential election. Here also only stories whose primary focus was the ex-presidents were analyzed. In all, a sample size of 380 stories was content–analyzed for this study. To determine reliability, the author and a separate coder together analyzed a random subsample of 10 percent (38) of the ex-presidential stories. There was a fairly good agreement on the categories between the two coders; reliability was 92.1 percent and was measured by dividing the number of agreed stories with total number of stories and then computing the percentage.

The study uses qualitative and quantitative data analyses to report its findings.

The use of qualitative and quantitative analyses leads to a broader interpretation or a more comprehensive look at the relationships between the ex-presidents and the press. Normal frequency distributions and chi-square analyses were used to empirically answer the research questions. In addition, inferential statistics were used to draw accurate, logical conclusions from data on all four ex-presidents.

ORGANIZATION OF THE BOOK

Life After the White House is organized in six chapters. Chapter 2 provides brief biographies of the ex-presidents, while Chapters 3 and 4 critically examine how each of the four ex-presidents was treated in the press during the immediate three years after he left the White House and political office. Chapter 5 provides a summary of the study and gives the overall picture of how the American press reported the activities of these elder statesmen. Specifically, it draws together the tone and major themes in the press coverage of ex-presidential news stories. This chapter also provides some concluding thoughts. Chapter 6 provides an annotated bibliography of books by and about the former presidents. The author's or publisher's own descriptions have been used to summarize the items in the selected bibliographies. Because of space constraints, several important works may have been left out here.

The study presents, for example, moments when each ex-president was honored and recognized for his important contributions to humanity and noble role in world affairs. Classic cases in point are when Reagan and Bush were individually honored as knights by the British Royal Crown or when, as early as August 1999, Ford and Carter received from President Clinton the nation's highest civilian honor, the Presidential Medal of Freedom. The study includes brief biographies about the ex-presidents and selected annotated books written by and about all four former U.S. presidents.

This study promises to whet public appetite for stories about America's most powerful and influential men. No other book or study presently deals with this subject specifically, that is, analysis of press coverage of ex-presidential news stories. Most books or research on American presidents and the kinds of relationship between them and the news media deal with their political lives while in office, not with their postoffice community and international service activities. However, the few books or studies that have touched on postpresidential activities of these elder statesmen do not specifically deal with ex-presidential–press relationships. This is definitely the first port of call for those seriously sailing or traveling the sea of knowledge seeking relevant information and materials about postpresidential years and activities of Ford, Carter, Reagan, and Bush.

The entries in this study were generated from computer-assisted literature searches from local public and university libraries in the Washington, D.C. area, research materials from the Presidential Libraries, and the Internet. Citations are mainly limited to quotations. Entries in the selected annotated bibliography section refer to books only.

The study serves as a very useful historic document and souvenir, depicting the private lives of four former American presidents of both major political parties as seen through the American press. Indeed, the study not only celebrates the lives and works of these elder statesmen but also pays glowing tribute to their selfless contributions to America and the world at large. In short, *Life After the White House* celebrates the American presidency. Also, this study celebrates America's emergence as the world's only superpower in the post–Cold War era—a feat unquestionably made possible through the power and influence of these past American leaders. This is a bipartisan book—an all-American book—that vividly depicts the continuing influences and works of these elder statesmen through the prism of the American press.

REFERENCES

Deakin, J. (1984). *Straight stuff: The reporters, the White House, and the truth.* New York: William Morrow.

Grossman, M. B., & Kumar, M. J. (1981). *Portraying the presidents: The White House and the news media.* Baltimore: Johns Hopkins University Press.

Harper, R. (1951). *Lincoln and the press.* New York: McGraw-Hill.

Johnston, A. (1990). Trends in political communication: A selective review of research in the 1980s. In David L. Swanson and Dan Nimmo (Eds.), *New direction in political communication: A resource book* (pp. 329–362). Newbury Park, CA: Sage.

Juergens, G. (1981). *News from the White House: The presidential–press relationship in the progressive era.* Chicago: University of Chicago Press.

Keogh, J. (1972). President Nixon and the press. New York: Funk & Wagnalls.

Lott, F. L. (1943). *Jefferson and the press.* Baton Rouge: Louisiana State University Press.

Pollard, J. (1947). *The president and the press.* New York: Macmillan.

Purvis, H. (Ed.). (1976). *The presidency and the press.* Austin: University of Texas at Austin.

Rozell, M. J. (1989). *The press and the Carter presidency.* Boulder, CO: Westview Press.

Rozell, M. J. (1992). *The press and the Ford presidency.* Ann Arbor: University of Michigan Press.

Rozell, M. J. (1996). *The press and the Bush presidency.* Westport, CT: Greenwood Press.

Rubin, R. (1981). *Press, party, and presidency.* New York: W. W. Norton.

Smith, C. (1990). *Presidential press conferences: A critical approach.* New York: Praeger.

Smoller, F. T. (1990). *The six o'clock presidency: A theory of presidential–press relations in the age of television.* New York: Praeger.

Stein, M. L. (1969). *When the presidents meet the press.* New York: Julian Messner.

Streitmatter, R. (1985, Spring). The impact of presidential personality on news coverage in major newspapers. *Journalism Quarterly*, 66–73.

Tebbel, J., & Watts, S. M. (1985). *The press and the presidency: From George Washington to Ronald Reagan*. New York: Oxford University Press.

Thompson, K. W. (1988). *The Ford presidency: Twenty-two intimate perspectives of Gerald Ford*. Lanham, MD: University Press of America.

White, G. (1979). *FDR and the press*. Chicago: University of Chicago Press.

Chapter 2

Brief Biographies of the Ex-Presidents

GERALD FORD (1974–1977)

Gerald R. Ford Jr., the 38th president of the United States, was the first to be inaugurated to that position without being elected. He was also the first nonelected vice president.

Ford was sworn in as president on August 9, 1974, after Richard M. Nixon resigned following the Watergate scandal. Ford was born Leslie Lynch King Jr. to Leslie Lynch King and Dorothy Ayer Gardner on July 14, 1913, in Omaha, Nebraska. Two weeks after his birth, his parents separated, and his mother took him to Grand Rapids, Michigan, to stay with her parents. His mother, Dorothy, remarried February 1, 1916, to Gerald R. Ford, a Grand Rapids paint and varnish salesman. The former president was then adopted by his stepfather and assumed his name. Ford became the half brother of Thomas, Richard, and James, living in an upper-middle-class home in the heartland of America. His earlier activities in Grand Rapids included active participation in the Boy Scouts of America and rising to the rank of Eagle Scout in November 1927.

Ford had his early education at South High School in Grand Rapids, where he excelled academically, earning him a name in the honor society. He earned honor, recognition, and placement on the "All-City" and "All-State" football teams because of his athletic capabilities. He won a football scholarship to attend the University of Michigan in Ann Arbor, between 1931 and 1935, majoring in economics and political science. Ford played on the university's national championship football teams and was voted the teams' Most Valuable Player in his senior year in 1934. He graduated with an economics degree in 1935.

Although Ford received offers to play professional football, he decided to take on a position as an assistant football and boxing coach at Yale University in

New Haven, Connecticut, because he intended to enter law school. He took courses part-time at Yale Law School because of his busy and hectic coaching responsibilities but eventually enrolled full-time, graduating in the top third of his class with a law degree in 1941. He then moved back to Grand Rapids to briefly practice law.

Ford went into partnership with his friend and college buddy Philip A. Buchen, who later served as his counsel in the White House. Ford also taught a business law course at the University of Grand Rapids and served as line coach for the school's football team. Furthermore, he took active part in the city's politics.

Ford enlisted in the U.S. Navy on April 20, 1942, where he had a four-year military career during World War II. In the navy, Ford continued his athletic pursuits. He was assigned to the navy's physical training unit and ended his career by directing that unit. He also served as an assistant navigational officer on the aircraft carrier *Monterey* with the U.S. Third Fleet based in the Pacific.

Ford was discharged honorably/victoriously from the navy as lieutenant commander in December 1945. He then returned to Grand Rapids to continue his law practice and to begin his political career in earnest. His first political encounter was with the incumbent Republican congressman Bartel J. Jonkman for the U.S. House of Representatives seat in Michigan's 5th District in the 1948 elections. Ford clinched the Republican nomination in September that year by a substantial margin and, on November 2 he was voted into Congress with a convincing victory. He served in the House of Representatives from January 3, 1949, to December 6, 1973.

Ford found time during the height of the 1948 campaign to marry his sweetheart, Elizabeth Ann Bloomer Warren, a department store fashion consultant. They subsequently were blessed with four children: Michael, John, Steven, and Susan.

While in Congress, Ford served, among other things, on the House Appropriations Committee and the Defense Appropriations Subcommittee and became the House Republican leader in January 1965. Earlier in 1961, he received the American Political Science Association's distinguished congressional service award.

Ford became popular among his peers as he moved from one congressional position to another. In fact, his longtime goal was to become Speaker of the House of Representatives, but this ambition was thwarted because the Republican Party did not get a majority in Congress. Instead, he was forced to settle for the position of minority leader.

Following the assassination of President John F. Kennedy in 1963, Lyndon Johnson, who took over the presidency, appointed Ford to serve on the Warren Commission, which investigated the assassination.

In October 1973, Ford's political career took an unexpected turn. After Vice President Spiro Agnew resigned unexpectedly after pleading no contest to charges of income tax evasion, President Nixon, acting under the 25th Amendment, selected Ford to replace him. In December the same year Ford won the confirmation in both the House and the Senate to became the nation's first nonelected vice president.

On August 9, 1974, Ford's political career took another turn. He became America's 38th president after Nixon was also forced to resign in the aftermath of the Watergate burglary scandal. This scandal stemmed from the break-in at the Democratic Party headquarters in the Watergate Hotel in downtown Washington, D.C., during the 1972 political campaign and the ensuing cover up by Nixon administration officials. Ford then nominated as vice president former New York governor Nelson A. Rockefeller, who was easily confirmed by Congress on December 19, 1974.

Precisely a month after Ford took the oath of office, he made the first critical decision that would later threaten his credibility and his presidency. On September 8, 1974, he granted Nixon "a full, free, and absolute pardon for all offenses against the United States." The American people disapproved of Ford's action. There were accusations from the media and from critics and opponents that Ford had a prearranged deal with Nixon to trade the presidency for a pardon. But he flatly and incessantly denied the existence of any such deal. "There was no deal, period, under no circumstances," he testified before Congress and maintained that the pardon was the right thing to do for the country. Ford had hoped that the Nixon pardon would heal the nation's political wounds and restore trust in the institution of the presidency after the divisive Vietnam War, but he was dead wrong.

To stem the growing tide of negative public reaction to the pardon and to appease one section of the populace, President Ford took the extraordinary steps of offering clemency to draft resisters and deserters from the Vietnam War. But this action was not enough. The cozy coverage that he had enjoyed in the media when he first came to power was no more; it had given way to severe, caustic media scrutiny and criticisms. The Nixon pardon haunted him to the very end of his presidency and undoubtedly cost him the 1976 presidential election for a secondterm in the White House. Ford, who chose Kansas senator Bob Dole as his running mate, lost to former Democratic governor of Georgia Jimmy Carter.

While Ford was in office, two women made assassination attempts on his life. Incidentally, both attempts occurred while he was on a trip to California in September 1975.

During his presidential tenure, Ford charted a conservative economic agenda. He told the nation that his "number-one priority" was to deal with inflation. He also promised to run an open and candid administration and to restore credibility in the American presidency. On the domestic front, Ford devoted much of his tenure to economic issues, particularly to shaping a sound fiscal policy. Among some of the major economic measures that he took were the stimulative tax cut, deregulation of regulatory agencies, and the fight for price stability. Although Ford favored a national energy policy based on the elimination of oil price controls, Congress opposed him, passing, instead, the Energy Policy and Conservation Act, which called for a gradual, phased decontrol to protect consumers.

On the foreign affairs front, Ford pursued Nixon's policy of détente with the Soviet Union, meeting occasionally with Premier Leonid Brezhnev to set new limitations on nuclear weapons, notably, SALT II. He also traveled to the Far East, especially Japan and China, to foster closer relationships with these countries. He maintained America's power and superiority after Cambodia and South Vietnam collapsed in early 1975. He ordered the evacuation of the last Americans from Saigon, now Ho Chin Minh City, as South Vietnam succumbed to the onslaught from Communist North Vietnam. Ford spent considerable time and effort to prevent the renewed outbreak of war in the Middle East.

Earlier in the fall of 1974, Ford's foreign policy suffered a setback after Congress passed an arms embargo against Turkey, which used American-made weapons to invade Cyprus. In May 1975, when Communist Cambodia captured an American merchant ship, the S.S. *Mayaguez*, and its 40-man crew in international waters, Ford immediately ordered American marines to rescue the ship and its crew and assault Cambodia. Although the military assault resulted in 41 American deaths, it provided opportunity for Ford to assert American superiority and to display presidential leadership. No wonder Americans rallied behind him, boosting his political image momentarily. Whatever his shortcomings, Ford managed to restore integrity and honor to the White House and to heal the nation by bringing it together and back on track.

When Gerald Ford left the White House on January 20, 1977, he and his wife, Elizabeth, better known as Betty, retired to their new home in Palm Springs, California. In 1981 the couple traveled around the world to several countries, including Singapore, Indonesia, Hong Kong, West Germany, France, Ireland, Japan, China, Oman, Abu Dhabi, Qatar, Britain, and Scandinavia. Then in October 1982 Ford and Betty traveled to Japan, where he spoke at a forum sponsored by Kansai Telecasting. In November 1985 Ford headed the U.S. delegation and served as the personal representative of the president of the United States to the 15th National Day celebrations of the sultanate of Oman.

Since leaving office, Ford has participated in several conferences and initiatives to bring about peace, harmony, and democracy in the world. He has collaborated with former president Jimmy Carter on several workshops and conferences, and the two even traveled together in April 1989 to monitor elections in Panama. The former president has received several national and international awards, including the Medal of Freedom in August 1999, America's highest civilian honor, presented to him by President Bill Clinton. In October 1999 Ford and Betty received the Congressional Gold Medal for "dedicated public services and outstanding humanitarian contributions." In December 1985 the U.S. Senate honored Ford by unveiling a marble bust of him in the halls of the Senate building for his role as president of the Senate while he was the vice president. Furthermore, several national and historic buildings, highways, and places have been named after Ford, including the University of Michigan's School of Public Policy. He also has received numerous honorary doctor of law degrees from various colleges and universities. In May 2001, the John F. Kennedy Library Foundation awarded Ford that year's Profile in Courage Award for taking the risk of pardoning Nixon in 1974 after the Watergate scandal. The award is given annually to an elected official who follows his or her conscience irrespective of the political consequence.

As an elder statesman, Ford continues to speak out on major issues concerning politics, both domestic and foreign. He also has been featured in news programs and documentaries for the National Broadcasting Company (NBC). Ford has appeared with other ex-presidents to support national issues, campaigns, and legislation in which they strongly believe, including NAFTA and America's permanent normal trade status with China. On late Tuesday, August 2, 2000, shortly after being honored at the Republican National Convention in Philadelphia Ford, 87, suffered a mild stroke and was admitted to the Hahnemann University Hospital. Later surgery was performed on his tongue to remove an abscess, and he was a few days later in excellent condition.

JIMMY CARTER (1977–1981)

James Earl Carter Jr., the 39th president of the United States, was born in Plains, Georgia, on October 1, 1924. The eldest of four children of James Earl Carter, a farmer and businessman, and Lillian Gordy Carter, a registered nurse, Jimmy Carter (who preferred Jimmy to James Earl) came from a family of conservative and evangelical background. The family's devout religious background, firmly grounded in the Baptist faith, shaped his upbringing and eventually his political career.

Carter had his early education at Plains High School and attended the Georgia Southwestern College and the Georgia Institute of Technology, where he excelled in mathematics and was accepted into the U.S. Naval Academy in Annapolis, Maryland, in 1946. He graduated in the top 10th of his class and later undertook graduate studies in nuclear physics at Union College, Schenectady, New York. After graduating from the academy, Carter married Rosalynn Smith, and they subsequently had four children, John William, James Earl III, Donnell Jeffrey, and Amy Lynn.

Carter served seven years as a naval officer, working on battleships and submarines and rising to the rank of lieutenant, which is a commissioned position. After his father died of cancer in 1953, Carter resigned his naval officer commission and returned to Plains to take over the family farm, expanding it to include a general-purpose seed and feed supply warehouse—and becoming a successful peanut farmer in the process.

Carter's initial political career started as a member and then chairman of the Sumter County School Board. He also became the first president of the Georgia Planning Association and president of the Georgia Crop Improvement Association.

Racial strife and upheaval in the South over the U.S. Supreme Court's May 1954 ruling *(Brown v. Board of Education of Topeka)* that school segregation was illegal fueled Carter's political ambition to run for the seat of the newly created 14th Senatorial District in Georgia during the legislative reapportionment of 1962. But his 1962 bid for the Georgia Senate run over a bump. After a long-, drawn-out legal battle over alleged voting irregularities and election fraud that showed that

Carter had lost the Democratic Party nomination election, a court-ordered recount placed him ahead of his opponent. He went on to clinch victory in the general election to serve two consecutive two-year terms in the Georgia Senate.

In 1966 Carter lost his first gubernatorial campaign but won the subsequent election in November 1970 to become the governor of Georgia on January 12, 1971. Because Carter was not eligible for a second term as governor, he immediately began preparation to run for the U.S. presidency after his term expired in January 1975. No doubt the political events of the 1962 campaign marked a turning point for Carter, shaping his political life and disposition to the electoral process.

On December 12, 1974, Carter announced his candidacy for U.S. president and launched an intensive two-year campaign, using grassroots organizations and canvassing strategies. He won the Democratic Party's nomination on the first ballot at the 1976 Democratic National Convention and chose Minnesota senator Walter F. Mondale as his running mate. Carter campaigned diligently against President Gerald Ford, pledging a more open government, preaching spiritual renewal, and promising that he would never lie to Americans. His campaign messages of openness, spiritual renewal, and morality resonated well with American voters, and he won the presidency on November 2, 1976, in one of the closest presidential elections in the nation's recent history.

Carter assumed the presidency on January 20, 1977, when the nation's economy was mired in rising inflation. He adopted several strategies to fight inflation by restraining public spending in order to keep budgets down. He started his belt-tightening economic measures within his own backyard—the White House—by reducing the staff by a third and ordering his cabinet staffers to drive their own cars. Carter also sold the presidential yacht and ended some of the presidential trappings of the presidency, including playing "Hail to the Chief" at his public ceremonies.

Carter came to office when the nation was faced with mounting inflation and unemployment. He worked incessantly to decrease the budget deficit and to increase job opportunities for Americans. He is credited by observers for the reformation of the civil service system and for appointing record numbers of women and minorities to government. He deregulated the trucking and airline industries and sought to protect the environment. He established a national energy policy and created the Department of Education to increase human and social services throughout the country. He expanded the U.S. national parks system and set aside for preservation roughly 103 million acres of Alaskan wilderness.

On the diplomatic front, Carter achieved many significant accomplishments. He successfully negotiated and got congressional approval for the Panama Canal Treaties of 1978 and represented the United States at the symbolic handover ceremony in mid-December 1999. The United States had run the Panama Canal, a strategic, 51-mile waterway, for nearly a century. He also was instrumental in the Camp David Treaty of March 1979, which sought peace between Israel and Egypt after 30 years of hostilities and bitter struggle. He also worked for stable and peaceful coexistence between Greece and Turkey. President Carter made diplomatic overtures to several Communist countries, including the People's Republic of China, Cuba, and Vietnam—and showed genuine devotion to détente and arms control. Carter provided U.S. support for the resistance movement in Afghanistan, strongly denounced the obnoxious apartheid policy in South Africa, and oversaw the transition of former Rhodesia (ruled by a white minority) to Zimbabwe (controlled by indigenous blacks). However, Carter's inability to amicably resolve the Iranian hostage crisis may have cost him the chance of being reelected in 1980. He was defeated by former Republican governor for California Ronald Reagan.

Since leaving office in January 1981, Carter has certainly become the busiest—and perhaps the most successful—of all the four former U.S. presidents. He has been traveling around the globe, resolving conflicts, exporting democracy, and fighting disease and poverty. He has brokered peace initiatives in several civil wars and internal conflicts in places such as Bosnia, Ethiopia, Haiti, North Korea, Somalia, and Sudan. He also has monitored democratic elections in the Dominican Republic, Guyana, Haiti, Jamaica, Liberia, Nicaragua, Panama, Paraguay, Zambia, and the West Bank/Gaza. In early July 2000 Carter was part of a team of international observers who witnessed the historic victory of the opposition Revolutionary Democratic Party in Mexico's presidential election after the 71-year hold of power by the ruling Institutional Revolutionary Party. Carter also has traveled extensively to Benin, Burundi, Burkina Faso, Ethiopia, Ghana, Kenya, Mali, Niger, Nigeria, Rwanda, Sudan, Togo, Uganda, and Zaire (now the Democratic Republic of Congo) to boost agriculture, eradicate diseases such as guinea worms, and promote peace and democracy.

Carter also has spent part of his postpresidency activities in creating opportunities for research and education. On October 29, 1981, the Carter Library was incorporated. The museum portion of the library was opened to visitors on October 1, 1986, and the library itself was opened to researchers on January 28, 1987. On October 2, 1984, groundbreaking work began for the Carter Center, which is a nonprofit organization designed to promote peace and human rights globally and was formally dedicated a year later on October 1, 1985. The center launched its Global 2000 Program, which seeks to foster improved education, agriculture, and health in developing countries. In August 1991 Carter announced the creation of the "Every Child by Two" project, which is a nationwide campaign for early childhood immunization. Then in September the center's Mental Health Task Force under the direction of Mrs. Rosalynn Carter was formed. On October 25, 1991, Carter announced the formation of The Atlanta Project (TAP), which is a major domestic initiative to address inner-city social problems related to poverty. In September 1992 Carter announced the creation of the center's new project called the Interfaith Health Resources Center, which is geared toward assisting faith-based organizations and groups in reaching disadvantaged populations with critical healthcare information. In November 1994 the Carter Center launched the "Not Even One" initiative to combat child deaths by firearms, and in January 1995 it launched the America Project to share with other cities strategies for urban revitalization developed by TAP.

Carter also has won several national and international recognitions for his work around the world. For example, in May 1981 he received the Truman Service Award for working quietly and persistently for the freedom of the 52 American hostages held in Tehran, Iran; in April 1990 he was awarded the Liberty Medal and cash prize of $100,000; and in October 1994 he received the J. William Fulbright Prize for International Understanding. As recently as August 1999, Carter and his wife, Rosalynn, received from President Bill Clinton the Medal of Freedom, which is the highest civilian honor in the United States.

Carter has been actively involved with Habitat for Humanity, a charitable organization that provides housing for the poor throughout the country. Furthermore, his activities with the Council of Freely Elected Heads of Government, the International Negotiating Network, and the International Human Rights Council are geared toward peace and democracy around the world. To date, Carter has traveled to more than 115 countries, spreading his message of peace, freedom, democracy, human rights, and disease eradication. After the contested 2000 presidential election, Carter and Ford, jointly chaired the bipartisan government-appointed National Commission on Federal Election Reform with a view to ensuring a modern and efficient electoral process in the country. In late July 2001, the commission submitted its report to President George W. Bush at a White House ceremony. Among its recommendations were: asking the media, especially the television networks, to refrain from calling elections until all polls are officially closed and making Election Day a national holiday.

RONALD REAGAN (1981–1989)

At age 69, Ronald Reagan on January 20, 1981, became the oldest person to occupy the U.S. presidency. He was born on February 6, 1911, in Tampico, Illinois, to Nelle, a Protestant, and John Edward Reagan, a Catholic. At the age of nine, his family moved to Dixon, a town where almost everybody knew one another. He entered Dixon High School at age 13 and, later, Eureka College, near his home, where he majored in economics. Reagan played football in high school and college and acted in college plays. He also was coach and captain of the Eureka College swimming team, which he helped create.

After graduating from college in June 1932, Reagan got a job as a radio sports announcer in Davenport, Iowa, and later in Des Moines. After a trip to California in 1937, Reagan managed to earn a contract with the Warner Brothers studios to feature in Hollywood movies. In all, he featured in 53 movies, making his last film in 1964. Among the movies he appeared in are *Kings Row, Knute Rockne—All American, The Last Outpost, Cattle Queen of Montana, The Voice of the Turtle, John Loves Mary, The Hasty Heart, The Winning Team,* and *The Killers.* Reagan interrupted his movie acting career in 1942 to serve for three years in the U.S. Army, where he made training films to boost the morale of soldiers and recruits.

Discharged from the army with the rank of captain, Reagan moved toward a political career. He chaired the Screen Actors Guild from 1947 to 1952 and managed to negotiate several of the guild's contracts. During his tenure he was embroiled in disputes and struggles over an attempted takeover/infiltration of Hollywood by Communist sympathizers. Although Reagan was a liberal Democrat, he became a dedicated Republican in 1960 after he came to the realization that Communism was infiltrating the nation's institutions and polity. Between 1954 and 1962, Reagan quit his movie career and served as a spokesperson for the General Electric Company, traveling all over the country and speaking about government intrusions and encroachments on the liberties and business lives of Americans. He also hosted the weekly television series called *General Electric Theater* on the Columbia Broadcasting System (CBS) network.

On March 4, 1952, Reagan, in the company of two close friends and a minister, married Nancy Davis, an actress, in the Little Brown Church in the San Fernando Valley, California. He had divorced his first wife, Jane Wyman, also an actress. Reagan has two children with Jane, Maureen and Michael (adopted), and two more with Nancy, Patricia Ann and Ronald Prescott.

Reagan's political career began with a 1964 television address sponsored by a Los Angeles automobile dealer that was designed to revive Senator Barry Goldwater's campaign for the presidency. His speech inspired a group of businessmen who suggested that he run for governor of California. On January 4, 1966, he announced his intention to seek the Republican nomination for governor and clinched the ticket with more than two-thirds of the vote. In the gubernatorial race, Reagan beat the Democratic Party incumbent Edmund G. Brown by an overwhelming margin and served two four-year terms.

In 1974 Reagan refused to run for a third term. Instead, he set his eyes on the U.S. presidency. But he failed to snatch the party's nomination from the Republican incumbent president Gerald R. Ford, who had succeeded to the presidency after Nixon resigned in the wake of the Watergate scandal. When Ford lost the 1976 presidential election to Jimmy Carter, the Democratic governor from Georgia, Reagan moved quickly to campaign for the 1980 Republican Party presidential nomination. On November 13, 1979, he declared himself candidate for president. He won the nomination and selected former Texas congressman George Bush as his running mate. Spiraling inflation, rising interest rates, high unemployment, and the taking of American hostages in Iran dogged Carter, leading demoralized Americans to vote overwhelmingly for Reagan, who won 489 of the 538 electoral votes.

On January 20, 1981, Reagan became the 40th president of the United States. Sixty-nine days later, March 30, Reagan survived an assassination attempt on his life in downtown Washington, D.C. A young, lone assailant by the name of John Hinckley Jr. pumped bullets into his chest, as well as into the head of his press secretary, the chest of a Secret Service agent, and the neck of a police officer. Reagan miraculously escaped the assassination attempt and made a remarkable recovery to serve his two-term presidency. In 1984 he and Vice President George Bush were reelected after defeating Democratic presidential contender Walter F. Mondale and running mate Geraldine Ferraro.

In his first presidential act, Reagan signed an executive order removing price controls on oil and gasoline to liberate the economy from excess government regulation. He also announced the release of 52 Americans held hostage in Iran, ending 444 days of captivity in the American Embassy in Tehran. He was able to work with Congress to seek legislation to control inflation and increase the number of Americans holding jobs, as well as strengthen America's defense capability. Reagan, classified as one of the most conservative U.S. presidents in recent history, drastically reduced government spending on social programs, but he increased defense spending exponentially, and by 1981 he proposed the Star Wars program, which sought to shield the United States from any missile attack from the Soviet Union or any enemy nation. In August 1981 President Reagan dismissed 11,438 members of the Professional Air Traffic Controllers Organization (PATCO) for walking off their jobs. Later in his presidency, on October 22, 1986, Reagan signed the comprehensive Tax Reform Act, which, among other things, sought to increase corporate taxes and reduce individual taxes.

In early November 1986, allegations surfaced that Reagan's administration had traded arms to Iran in exchange for American hostages in Beruit and that profits from the arms sales were diverted to the Contra rebels in Nicaragua. This revelation triggered congressional hearings, which resulted in the indictment in 1988 of key administration officials.

On the international front, Reagan espoused a doctrine that branded the Soviet Union as the "evil empire" and sought to check that country's expansionism throughout the world. However, he managed to work cooperatively with Soviet leader Mikhail Gorbachev to finalize the Intermediate-Range Nuclear Forces (INF) Treaty in Moscow, which would ban all short- and medium-range nuclear missiles in Europe.

On October 25, 1983, he deployed American troops into Grenada to rescue American students and to halt the forces of tyranny and maintain stability in that Caribbean island nation. Furthermore, in mid-April 1986 Reagan ordered air strikes against Libya for attacking American planes in international waters and for its alleged complicity in the bombing of a disco in West Berlin that killed two U.S. soldiers, a Turkish woman, and injured several others. In 1988 Reagan created the 14th cabinet post, the Department of Veterans Affairs, to cater to the needs and interests of America's war veterans.

At the time Reagan left office on January 20, 1989, America was strong, and Americans generally felt good about themselves and their country. He and his wife, Nancy, flew on the airplane Air Force One to California to begin their private lives. In June 1989 Reagan traveled to London to give the Winston Churchill Lecture to the English-Speaking Union and received honorary knighthood from Queen Elizabeth II. During this European trip, he stopped over in Paris, France, where he was inducted into the Academy of Moral and Political Science and celebrated the 100th anniversary of the Eiffel Tower.

Nine months after leaving office, Reagan in October 1989 embarked on a two-day trip to Japan, where he received a medal, the Grand Cordon of the Supreme Order of the Chrysanthemum, from the Japanese government. During his trip he urged Japan to open its markets to more U.S. imports and to step up its aid to the world's poorest nations.

In September 1990 the Reagans embarked on a 10-day, four-nation European trip that took them to East and West Germany, Poland, and the Soviet Union. The trip provided Reagan the opportunity to assess firsthand democratic transformations and recent political events in that part of the world. Before returning to the United States, Reagan made a stopover in the Vatican City for an audience with Pope John Paul II.

On November 4, 1991, the Ronald Reagan Presidential Library was dedicated in Simi Valley, California, to preserve documents and memorabilia from the Reagan administration. In the early part of his retirement years, Reagan traveled the country and around the world to deliver speeches and to accept international awards. For example, he spoke at the University of California, Los Angeles, in February 1989, spoke at several business meetings in Japan in October that same year, addressed the Oxford Union Society in England in December 1992, and addressed the Polish Parliament in September 1994.

In January 1993 Reagan and Jimmy Carter were named joint recipients of the first Spark M. Matsunaga Medals for Peace award, and President George Bush awarded Reagan the Presidential Medal of Freedom. Earlier, in May 1992, Reagan presented the first Ronald Reagan Freedom Award to Soviet leader Mikhail Gorbachev, and in November 1993 he presented the second Reagan Freedom Award to General Colin L. Powell (ret.), former Joint Chiefs of Staff chairman, at the White House. Reagan, like his predecessors, supports numerous charitable causes nationally and internationally, for example, his help in easing the pain of the 1993 earthquake victims in southern California.

In early November 1994 Reagan in a moving letter to Americans revealed that he had been diagnosed with Alzheimer's disease, a terrible degenerative ailment that affects memory. According to the letter, he and wife, Nancy, had decided to make the revelation in the hopes that more public attention would be focused on the disease and bring about a better understanding of its effects on individuals and families who are affected by it. Subsequently, Reagan has been absent from the public eye. Nevertheless, in early March 2001 a new nuclear-powered aircraft carrier, U.S.S. *Ronald Reagan*, was named after the former president at a christening ceremony at the Newport News shipbuilding yard in Virginia.

GEORGE BUSH (1989–1993)

The 41st U.S. president, George Herbert Walker Bush was born in Milton, Massachusetts, on June 12, 1924, to Dorothy and Prescott Bush, an affluent investment banker and Republican senator from Connecticut between 1952 and 1963. The young Bush grew up in Greenwich, Connecticut, where he attended the County Day School and later Phillips Academy in Andover, Massachusetts.

Bush enlisted in the U.S. Navy on his 18th birthday, becoming the youngest pilot to receive his wings at the time. During World War II, Bush flew 58 combat missions and was once shot down by Japanese antiaircraft fire over the Pacific Ocean and rescued by the navy submarine U.S.S. *Finback*. For bravery in action, Bush received the Distinguished Flying Cross and three Air Medals.

On January, 6, 1945, Bush married Barbara Pierce, daughter of a magazine publisher. They had six children—George (now America's 43rd president), Robbin, John (also known as Jeb and now Florida governor), Neil, Marvin, and Dorothy.

In 1948 Bush graduated Phi Beta Kappa from Yale University with a bachelor's degree in economics. While in college he captained the baseball team and was a member of the college's exclusive fraternity, the Skull and Bones Society.

Bush started his business career in West Texas, where he worked for Dresser Industries, an oil-field supply company, as a trainee and oil supply salesman. In 1951 he cofounded the small royalty firm Bush-Overbey Oil Development Company. Then in 1953 he cofounded the Zapata Petroleum Corporation and in 1954 became president of its subsidiary, the Zapata Off-Shore Company, which drilled oil for major distributors on contract. When the subsidiary became independent in 1958, Bush moved its headquarters from Midland, Texas, to Houston, serving as its president until 1964, then as its chairperson until 1966. He sold his shares in the company for good profit to enter politics.

Initially, Bush served as chairperson of the Harris County Republican Party. He first attempted to run for the office of U.S. senator in 1964 but lost to Democratic incumbent Ralph Yarborough. Undeterred by this defeat, Bush in 1966 ran for a seat in the House of Representatives from Texas' 7th District and won this time, as the first Republican to represent Houston. Bush was reelected in 1968. Bush again tried to capture the Senate seat in 1970 and faced formidable opponent Lloyd M. Bentsen, who won handily.

Between 1971 and 1977 Bush served in several high-level positions in the government and in the Republican Party. In February 1971 President Nixon appointed him as U.S. ambassador to the United Nations, and later in October 1974 he moved to Beijing to serve as chief of the U.S. Liaison Office in the People's Republic of China. In January 1973 Bush became chairperson of the Republican National Committee and in January 1976 was appointed by President Gerald Ford to head the Central Intelligence Agency (CIA).

In early 1977 Bush moved back to Houston to return to private life. Two years later he announced his candidacy for the U.S. presidency. Although Bush campaigned vigorously for the Republican nomination in 1980, he lost to former California governor Ronald Reagan, who later chose him as his vice presidential running mate.

The Reagan–Bush Republican ticket won the presidential election, beating the Democratic ticket of Carter–Mondale by an overwhelming margin. In 1988 Bush won the Republic nomination for president, and, with Indiana senator Dan Quayle as his running mate, he defeated the Democratic team of Massachusetts governor Michael Dukakis and Texas senator Lloyd Bentsen in the general election.

Bush came to office at a time when the Cold War, which began in 1945 and divided the world between East and West, was gradually coming to a close, with the collapse of the former Soviet Union, the tearing down of the Berlin Wall, and the reunification of East and West Germany. Bush is credited for presiding successfully over the collapse of totalitarianism and the emergence of true democracy in Eastern Europe.

In September 1990 he managed a bipartisan federal budget agreement that broke a budget deadlock and served as the first move toward reducing the federal deficit. He pushed for new ideas for educational reform, homeownership financing, and environmental protection.

While in office, Bush signed three major pieces of legislation, notably, the Americans with Disabilities Act on July 26, 1990, the Clean Air Act on November 15, 1990, and the Civil Rights Act on November 21, 1991. The Disabilities Act bars discrimination against nearly 43 million Americans with physical and mental disabilities and attacks the problem of "hate crimes" in America; the Clean Air Act seeks to sharply reduce pollution from automobiles and factories; and the Civil Rights Act significantly strengthens civil rights protection in the country. The civil rights and the clean air acts were the reauthorization versions of existing laws.

On the international front, Bush made several diplomatic trips to Russia, Poland, and Hungary to meet with their leaders to foster understanding and cooperation between these countries and the United States. For example, he met with Russian leader Mikhail Gorbachev in July 1991 to sign the strategic arms limitation talks (START I), which seeks to reduce the strategic nuclear forces of the two countries, and had another meeting in January 1993 with Boris Yeltsin to sign the second arms talks (START II). Bush also took several military actions against two countries to send a clear message that the United States would not tolerate authoritarianism and dictatorship. For example, on December 30, 1989, he launched military action against Panama to restore democracy and to capture its leader, Samuel Noriega, accused of dictatorship and international drug trafficking. Also, on January 16, 1991, Bush ordered the beginning of Operation Desert Storm to liberate Kuwait from Iraqi military occupation. In early December 1992 he announced Operation Restore Hope to relieve starvation in Somalia. He worked diligently to get Canada and Mexico to approve a draft of the North American Free Trade Agreement in 1992. Although Bush pushed for a "new world order," he is criticized for not being aggressive enough with his newfound vision.

After leaving the White House on January 20, 1993, George Bush and wife, Barbara, returned to private life in Houston, Texas. On November 6, 1997, the George Bush Library and Museum was opened on the campus of the Texas A&M University, College Station. The library and museum contains materials and information that one might need to know about the 41st president's life and public career.

Bush serves as the honorary chairman of the board of directors of the Points of Light Foundation. He also supports several charity and volunteer groups and organizations. Bush and his wife, Barbara, serve on the Board of Visitors of M.D. Anderson Hospital. Bush serves on the board of the Episcopal Church Foundation and on the vestry of St. Ann's Episcopal Church in Kennebunkport, Maine.

REFERENCES

Brinkley, A., & Dyer, D. (Eds.). (2000). *The reader's companion to the American presidency*. Boston: Houghton Mifflin.
http://gi.grolier.com/presidents/ea/bios/39pcart.html
http://bushlibrary.tamu.edu/biography/president/bio.html
http://gi.grolier.com/presidents/ea/bios/41pbush.html
http://gi.grolier.com/presidents/ea/bios/40preag.html
www.ibjlib.utexas.edu/ford/grf/fordbio.htm
www.ipl.org/ - = - potus@ipl.org
www.whitehouse.gov/WH/glimpse/html/gb41.html
www.whitehouse.gov/WH/glimpse/html/rr40.html
www.whitehouse.gov/WH/glimpse/html/jc39.html

∼ Chapter 3 ∼

Quantitative Results
and Discussion

This chapter reports the quantitative results of this study, depicting the relative emphasis the three elite American newspapers placed on the coverage of ex-presidents Gerald Ford, Jimmy Carter, Ronald Reagan, and George Bush. It also shows the types of stories published and their tone. Of the overall sample size of 380 stories analyzed—that is, about one-fourth of all ex-presidential stories in the three newspapers for the years covered—Table 3.1 shows that the *Washington Post* published 41.1 percent (156) of the stories, the *Los Angeles Times* carried 36.1 percent (137), and the *New York Times* ran 22.9 percent (87). The margin of sample error for overall results is plus or minus four percentage points.

TABLE 3.1
Distribution of Ex-Presidential Stories by Newspaper

NEWSPAPER	FREQUENCY	PERCENT
New York Times	87	22.9
Washington Post	156	41.1
Los Angeles Times	137	36.1
TOTAL	380	100.0

As Table 3.2 indicates, Ford received the highest coverage of 31.6 percent (120 stories), followed by Ronald Reagan with 30.0 percent (114 stories), Jimmy Carter with 27.9 percent (106 stories), and, finally, George Bush with the lowest coverage at 10.5 percent (40 stories). It is important to note that press coverage was extremely heavy in the first year after each president left office. First, the amount of press coverage that an ex-president receives largely depends on the type of postpresidential schedule that he draws up after leaving office. An ex-president has to be active in order to become an important "continuing story." For example, Ford received the highest coverage in 1977 with 17.6 percent of the stories focusing on him, Reagan followed with 16.6 percent in 1989, Carter was next with 13.2 percent in 1981, and Bush with only 7.1 percent in 1993 (see Table 3.3).

Roughly 64 days after vacating the Oval Office, Ford was back in Washington, D.C., meeting with his former cabinet members, the Republican congressional leadership, and incumbent president Jimmy Carter at the White House and speaking at a luncheon of the American Enterprise Institute. He also accepted several job offers, including a television network position, commenting on documentaries relating to the presidency. So Ford kept himself extremely busy and as a result was constantly in the news.

Reagan also received notable press coverage in his early retirement years, particularly between 1989 and 1990, but most of his coverage centered on the Iran–Contra trial. His early postpresidential schedule also included an appearance at the 60th "All-Star" baseball game in Anaheim, California, in July 1989, at which he announced the game sitting side by side with NBC commentator Vin Sculley, and foreign trips to England and Japan. Also, Reagan made another public appearance in late November 1989 to attend a political fund-raising dinner for California gubernatorial candidate U.S. senator Pete Wilson.

On his part, Carter, it is fair to say, did not finish his presidential duties when he relinquished the official reins of power on January 20, 1981. At President Reagan's request, Carter traveled to Wiesbaden, West Germany—accompanied by his vice president, Walter Mondale, and other high-level U.S. officials—to meet the 52 freed American hostages who were held in Iran for 444 days. This trip no doubt served as a stepping-stone for Carter, who subsequently embarked on elaborate diplomatic and humanitarian efforts to resolve conflicts, promote democracy,

TABLE 3.2
Distribution of Stories by Ex-Presidents

PRESIDENT	FREQUENCY	PERCENT
Ford	120	31.6
Carter	106	27.9
Reagan	114	30.0
Bush	40	10.5
TOTAL	**380**	**100.0**

TABLE 3.3
Distribution of Ex-Presidential Stories by Time Period

YEAR OF PUBLICATION	FREQUENCY	PERCENT
FORD		
1977	67	17.6
1978	31	8.2
1979	22	5.8
CARTER		
1981	50	13.2
1982	27	7.1
1983	29	7.6
REAGAN		
1989	62	16.3
1990	33	8.7
1991	19	5.0
BUSH		
1993	27	7.1
1994	7	1.8
1995	6	1.6
TOTAL	**380**	**100.0**

and foster economic development throughout the world. As Douglas Brinkley (1998) writes: "He knew he wanted to do a lot more than build a museum-library in tribute of himself and give a lot of after-dinner speeches. What Carter really wanted was to find some way to continue the unfinished business of his presidency, and he made this no secret from the start" (p. xvi).

For Bush, two months after he left the White House, he was back in the news as he went to Washington to receive an award from the National Security Industrial Association, a group of major defense contractors. Then in early April 1993 he and wife, Barbara, traveled to Kuwait at the invitation of the emir, where he was honored for helping to free that country from Iraqi occupation in 1991. Bush was in the news again in September, when he returned to Washington to join Carter in the White House signing of the framework for Middle East peace and to throw their weight and support behind congressional passage of NAFTA. After these public appearances, however, Bush maintained a low profile and stayed out of the limelight.

Research questions 1 and 2 asked, How much press coverage is given to the ex-presidents? and What is the nature of the relationship between the press and the four ex-presidents? From the evidence, it is absolutely clear that the first year of an ex-president's leaving office represents a high point in his life as he makes the transition from president to private citizen. Obviously, at this early transitional stage, the press is keenly interested in knowing what the ex-president is doing in retirement and how he is adjusting to his new life. Once this curiosity is satisfied, the number of news stories progressively declines over time (again, see Table 3.3). Generally, the amount of press coverage that an ex-president receives depends to a large extent on how he wants to spend the rest of his life: either take it easy and avoid media spotlights or continue working toward goals in which he believes in the hopes of drawing both media and public attention to them. Certainly, an ex-president with a rigorous agenda is bound to capture more media attention than one with a less rigorous postpresidential schedule. This study provides clear evidence demonstrating that the ex-presidents continue to receive press coverage, even though they are officially out of office, but the degree of coverage is dependent on how busy that particular ex-president is and how much media contact he initiates as a result. Thus, the relationship between the press and the ex-presidents depends in great measure upon each individual's level of postpresidential activity. No more do they automatically attract media attention, especially if they are inactive. In most instances the press can do little until the ex-president initiates action or media contact. This means that, once out of office, the ex-presidents have considerable control over the way that the press covers them.

Table 3.4 provides a breakdown of what types of ex-presidential stories were most frequently used in the three American newspapers studied. An overwhelming 275 (72.4 percent) were straight news stories, 61 (16.1 percent) were feature articles or commentaries, and only 9 (2.4 percent) were editorials. Also, book reviews and cartoons each were carried 12 times (3.2 percent), and letters to the editor were published 11 times (2.9 percent). The news stories published varied from how the ex-presidents were adjusting to their new private lives, to the several vacations and foreign trips that they were taking, to their appearances at party fund-raising and award ceremonies. Overall, the *Washington Post* published 100 news stories, the *Los Angeles Times* carried 98, and *New York Times* ran 77. Again the *Post* lead in the number of feature articles that dealt with the ex-presidents. It carried 36 articles, the *Los Angeles Times* published 20, and the *New York Times* ran only 5. Regarding editorial opinions, the *Los Angeles Times* published the highest of 6 and the *Post* and the *New York Times* each carried 2. Chi-square analysis indicates significant differences between the newspapers and the types of stories they each published ($X^2 = 27.87913$, df = 10, p<.00189). This result suggests that all three newspapers placed considerably more emphasis on regular news stories than on the remaining four types of stories or news presentation styles.

TABLE 3.4
Distribution of Story Type by Newspaper

STORY TYPE	NEW YORK TIMES		WASHINGTON POST		LOS ANGELES TIMES		TOTAL	
	#	%	#	%	#	%	#	%
News Story	76	20.0	100	26.3	98	25.8	274	72.1
Editorial	2	0.5	2	0.5	6	1.6	10	2.6
Feature	5	1.3	36	9.5	20	5.3	61	16.1
Letter to the Editor	2	0.5	6	1.6	3	0.8	11	2.9
Book Review	2	0.5	8	2.1	2	0.5	12	3.2
Cartoon	0	0.0	4	1.1	8	2.1	12	3.2
TOTAL	**87**	**22.9**	**156**	**41.1**	**137**	**36.1**	**380**	**100.0**

NOTE: $X^2 = 27.87913$, df $= 10$, p $<.00189$.

Research question 3 asked, What are the nature and treatment of ex-presidential issues in the American press? This question is answered by the data in Tables 3.5 and 3.6. As seen in Table 3.5, an overwhelming majority of the stories ran in the inside pages rather than on the front pages of the three newspapers. Reagan received the largest number of inside-page stories (106), followed by Ford (104), Carter (93), then Bush (37). Of those stories published on the front pages, Ford received the highest of 16, Carter had the next highest of 13, and Reagan had 8 stories. Bush had only 3 front-page stories. Carter hit the front pages of the *Los Angeles Times* in 11 of the cases, but the *New York Times* only twice. Ford, on his part, captured the front pages of both the *Washington Post* and the *Los Angeles Times* in 6 of the cases. Reagan appeared on the front pages of the *Post* on five

TABLE 3.5
Number and Placement of Ex-Presidential Stories in Three American Newspapers

NEWSPAPER	FORD		CARTER		REAGAN		BUSH	
	Front	Inside	Front	Inside	Front	Inside	Front	Inside
New York Times	4	35	2	20	0	14	1	11
Washington Post	6	40	0	35	5	51	2	17
Los Angeles Times	6	29	11	38	3	41	0	9
TOTAL	**16**	**104**	**13**	**93**	**8**	**106**	**3**	**37**

N=380.
All figures represent number of stories.

occasions and in the *Los Angeles Times* three times. The few stories that gained prominence in the front pages primarily focused on White House departures after serving an official term, personal interviews, and opening of presidential museums/libraries. As expected, the bulk of the inside-page stories comprised editorials, features, letters, book reviews, cartoons, and all the other small news stories. Only those stories that the newspaper deemed important made it to the front pages.

Table 3.6 shows the length of the stories that each newspaper published about the ex-presidents. A majority of the long stories focused on Reagan (43), with the *Washington Post* publishing the most (27 stories). Ford received the next most lengthy stories (13), again with the *Post* publishing the most (7 stories). Bush received the third largest number of long stories (11), with the *Post* publishing the most (8). Overall, Carter had the lowest number of long stories (6). The bulk of the medium-length stories dealt with both Ford and Reagan, who each had 58, followed in that descending order by Carter (55) and Bush (23). In the small-length subcategory, the *New York Times* ran the majority, focusing largely on Ford (22 stories). The *Post* carried 19 short or brief stories about Carter, the *New York Times* ran 15 stories, and the *Los Angeles Times* published 11 short stories. The *New York Times* published 22 short or brief stories about Ford, the *Los Angeles Times* published 18, and the *Post* ran only 9 about him.

TABLE 3.6
Number and Length of Ex-Presidential Stories in Three American Newspapers

NEWSPAPER	FORD			CARTER			REAGAN			BUSH		
	S	M	L	S	M	L	S	M	L	S	M	L
New York Times	22	15	2	15	7	0	6	8	0	5	5	2
Washington Post	9	30	7	19	13	3	1	28	27	1	10	8
Los Angeles Times	18	13	4	11	35	3	6	22	16	0	8	1
TOTAL	**49**	**58**	**13**	**45**	**55**	**6**	**13**	**58**	**43**	**6**	**23**	**11**

N=380.
NOTES: **S** = small; **M** = medium; **L** = long. All figures represent number of stories.

Research question 4 asked, What is the general tone of news items on these four U.S. ex-presidents? Tables 3.7, 3.8, 3.9, and 3.10 address this question. Table 3.7 indicates that half of the stories (50.3 percent) were favorable to the ex-presidents, a third (34.2 percent) were neutral, and a few (15.5 percent) were unfavorable. Chi-square analysis shows significant differences among the tone of the stories and the ex-presidents ($X^2 = 17.63978$, df = 6, p <.00720).

TABLE 3.7
Comparative Evaluation of Tone of Ex-Presidential Stories in
Three American Newspapers

EX-PRESIDENT	FAVORABLE		NEUTRAL		UNFAVORABLE		TOTAL	
	#	%	#	%	#	%	#	%
Ford	64	16.8	42	11.1	14	3.7	120	31.6
Carter	58	15.3	38	10.0	10	2.6	106	27.9
Reagan	44	11.6	41	10.8	29	7.6	114	30.0
Bush	25	6.6	9	2.4	6	1.6	40	10.5
TOTAL	**191**	**50.3**	**130**	**34.2**	**59**	**15.5**	**380**	**100.0**

NOTE: $X^2 = 17.63978$, df = 6, p <.00720.

The breakdown of the results, as indicated in Table 3.8, reveals that, overall, Ford received the highest number of favorable coverage (64 stories), followed in descending order by Carter (58 stories), Reagan (44 stories), and Bush (25 stories). When straight news stories were considered in terms of their neutrality to the ex-presidents, the highest of 25 went to Reagan, the second highest of 24 went to both Ford and Carter, and the lowest of 8 went to Bush. Reagan had considerably more favorable feature articles about him (6) than the other three ex-presidents. Carter received 3, and Ford had only 1 under the feature subcategory. Ford led in the number of neutral feature articles about the ex-presidents with 13, followed by Reagan with 12. Most of these articles offered a well-balanced and objective assessment of the ex-president in question. The main reason that there were so many neutral stories is that the newspapers did well in balancing most of their stories by providing background and setting, which invariably produced fairly balanced stories.

Overall, there was more favorable press coverage in the straight news story subcategory for Ford (61) than there was for Carter (48), Reagan (34), and Bush (23). Reagan received more unfavorable editorial comments (5) than the rest of the ex-presidents combined but had 1 favorable comment about him. None of the others received any positive editorial comment. Book reviews in the three newspapers slightly favored Carter over Reagan and Ford. The story sample for the period studied did not include any book reviews about Bush. Of the six letters written mostly about Carter, 3 were classified as favorable and the other 3 were coded as neutral. Ford and Reagan each had 1 favorable letter written about him. Regarding cartoons, the negative category was overwhelming, especially for Reagan (7), followed by Carter (2). These editorial cartoons satirized and caricatured the two ex-presidents.

TABLE 3.8
Type and Tone of Ex-Presidential Stories in Three American Newspapers

STORY TYPE	FORD			CARTER			REAGAN			BUSH		
	+	0	-	+	0	-	+	0	-	+	0	-
News Story	61	24	6	48	24	7	34	25	11	23	8	3
Editorial	0	1	1	0	1	0	1	1	5	0	0	0
Feature	1	13	4	3	9	1	6	12	6	2	1	3
Letter to the Editor	1	0	2	3	3	0	1	1	0	0	0	0
Book Review	1	3	1	4	0	0	2	1	0	0	0	0
Cartoon	0	1	0	0	1	2	0	1	7	0	0	0
TOTAL	**64**	**42**	**14**	**58**	**38**	**10**	**44**	**41**	**29**	**25**	**9**	**6**

N=380.
NOTES: + = favorable; 0 = neutral; - = unfavorable. All figures represent number of stories.

As shown in Table 3.9, a majority of the favorable stories about Ford (25) came from the *New York Times* and those about Carter (21) came from the *Los Angeles Times*. The *Washington Post* also gave Ford the most favorable stories (19), while it gave Carter and Reagan 18 favorable stories each and Bush only 10 favorable stories. Ironically, although the *Post* gave Reagan the most favorable coverage, the same newspaper gave him the most unfavorable coverage (16 stories). While the number of favorable stories was 20 for Ford in the *Los Angeles Times*, the number of his unfavorable stories was only 7 in the same newspaper. Also, while the *New York Times* ran 7 favorable stories about Bush, it gave him only 2 unfavorable stories in the sample analyzed for this study. Certainly, it was no accident that, in terms of the nature and extent of press coverage that each

TABLE 3.9
Number and Tone of Ex-Presidential Stories in Three American Newspapers

NEWSPAPER	FORD			CARTER			REAGAN			BUSH		
	+	0	-	+	0	-	+	0	-	+	0	-
New York Times	25	12	2	19	3	0	11	3	0	7	3	2
Washington Post	19	22	5	18	13	4	18	22	16	10	6	3
Los Angeles Times	20	8	7	21	22	6	15	16	13	8	0	1
TOTAL	**64**	**42**	**14**	**58**	**38**	**10**	**44**	**41**	**29**	**25**	**9**	**6**

N=380.
NOTES: + = favorable; 0 = neutral; - = unfavorable. All figures represent number of stories.

president received, Bush received the lowest number of stories, overall, at least three times less than Carter, who placed third. Bush was conspicuously out of the news most of the time, hence, his low press coverage figures (see also Table 3.2).

If one looks at Table 3.10, one notices that most of the unfavorable stories (13) emerged from the politics and judiciary subcategories under Reagan. The newspapers were particularly critical of some of Reagan's political decisions while in office and about his involvement in the Iran–Contra arms for hostages deal. Although most of the stories dealing with judiciary issues were neutral and well balanced, some were critical of Reagan's role in the Iran–Contra affair. In fact, the heavy press coverage of this affair and its subsequent court battles compelled presidential historian Haynes Johnson to argue in a *Washington Post* article that Ronald Reagan, not Oliver North, was on trial in his (North's) criminal trial. Johnson referred to North's lawyer, Brenden V. Sullivan Jr., noting, "In defending North and depicting him as a loyal subordinate faithfully carrying out the wishes of his superiors, he has in effect placed Reagan on trial." Johnson concludes that the peril of the trial was not to U.S. security or America's international relations but to Reagan's reputation and standing in history (see Johnson's article in the *Washington Post* of March 3, 1989, p. A2).

It should be noted that the ex-presidents contributed somehow to the upsurge of negative stories about themselves in the newspapers. In some of the stories analyzed, they attacked one another's policies and actions. For example, after Ford left office, he criticized the Carter administration's anti-inflation efforts, while Carter, once out of office, attacked Reagan's economic policies.

Under the subcategory recreation/vacation, Carter received more favorable coverage (14) than Ford (8), Reagan (7), and Bush (3). Carter, for example, made several vacation trips that received widespread press coverage. Also his affinity with the outdoors and fly-fishing contributed to his favorability in this subcategory. Under the awards/honors subcategory, Reagan had the most favorable stories (10), followed by Ford (8), Bush (5), and Carter (4). Reagan, the most popular and longest serving of the four, received several awards, commendations, and honorary degrees in recognition of his strong leadership and vigorous efforts in almost single-handedly ending the Cold War and making America the world's only superpower today.

Regarding education issues, Ford topped the rest with 10 favorable stories as he shuttled from one university campus to another across the nation in his newfound role as an "itinerant professor," sharing his visions and thoughts about America and the presidency with students. Also under this subcategory, Reagan received 9 favorable stories, Carter 6, and Bush 3. The newspapers had more highly favorable coverage of Ford (6) on economy than of Carter (3) and Bush (3). Reagan did not have any favorable rating here. Also, the newspapers gave Carter a more favorable rating on health issues than they did the other ex-presidents.

TABLE 3.10

Subject Category and Tone of Ex-Presidential Stories in Three American Newspapers

SUBJECT CATEGORY	FORD +	FORD 0	FORD -	CARTER +	CARTER 0	CARTER -	REAGAN +	REAGAN 0	REAGAN -	BUSH +	BUSH 0	BUSH -
Awards/Honors	8	0	0	4	1	0	10	0	0	5	0	0
Recreation/Vacation	8	2	0	14	1	0	7	0	0	3	0	0
Politics	30	25	9	26	26	7	14	10	13	8	4	2
Economy	6	6	4	3	5	1	0	5	2	3	2	0
Health	1	5	1	5	0	1	1	2	0	0	0	0
Education	10	2	0	6	1	1	9	4	0	3	1	0
Judiciary	0	2	0	0	3	0	3	20	13	3	2	4
Other	1	0	0	0	1	0	0	0	1	0	0	0
TOTAL	64	42	14	58	38	10	44	41	30	25	9	6

N=380.

NOTES: + = favorable; 0 = neutral; - = unfavorable. All figures represent number of stories.

In summary, the data provided in this chapter tried to answer four key re-search questions posed by this study: (1) How much press coverage is given to the ex-presidents? (2) What is the nature of the relationship between the press and the four ex-presidents? (3) What are the nature and treatment of ex-presidential issues in the American press? (4) What is the general tone of news items on these four U.S. ex-presidents? The results show that the *Washington Post* had much of the coverage about the ex-presidents (41.1 percent), followed by the *Los Angeles Times* (36.1 percent), and then the *New York Times* (22.9 percent). Overall, Ford had the most extensive coverage among the four ex-presidents, apparently because he was more vigorous initially when he left the White House than the other ex-presidents, with Bush obtaining the least. The study found that the newspapers would empha-size straight news stories over the other five story-type categories: editorial, fea-ture/commentary, letter to the editor, book review, and cartoon. The overwhelming majority of the stories appeared in the inside pages, and they were mostly medium in length. The tone of the stories was generally favorable to the ex-presidents, with Ford again receiving the highest, followed by Carter, Reagan, and Bush in that order. Where the story was not favorable, the tone was generally more neutral than negative. The study suggests that having more press coverage requires the initia-tive of the ex-president himself to get his views and activities into the press. If he does not want to be bothered, the press stands little chance of intruding into his privacy. Thus, the relationship between the press and the ex-presidents is largely based on mutual respect and less media intrusion. Specifically, this relationship is much more cordial and less adversarial than when the men were chief executives with tremendous policy and decision-making powers. After retirement, the ex-president determines the extent of press coverage that he desires, not the press.

REFERENCES

Brinkley, D. (1998). *The unfinished presidency: Jimmy Carter's journey beyond the White House.* New York: Viking Press.

Johnson, H. (March 3, 1989). Vantage point at the North trial. *Washington Post,* p. A2.

— Chapter 4 —

Qualitative Results
and Analyses

This section of the study analyzes stories to determine how the ex-presidents were covered and treated in the three elite American newspapers: the *Los Angeles Times*, the *New York Times*, and the *Washington Post*. In all, 48 out of a total of 380 stories that primarily focused on Presidents Gerald Ford, Jimmy Carter, Ronald Reagan, and George Bush were randomly selected for qualitative analyses. Specifically, each news story was assigned a number, and then the numbers were placed in a tray, grouped by each ex-president. Finally, a total of 48, representing 12 for each ex-president, was randomly selected for qualitative analyses. The stories were published during these periods: Ford, 1977–1979; Carter, 1981–1983; Reagan, 1989–1991; and Bush, 1993–1995. The qualitative analysis helps to a greater extent in determining the level, tone, and extent of coverage of ex-presidential stories in all three newspapers studied.

PORTRAIT OF FORD IN THE PRESS

January 30, 1977. The story in this day's issue of the *New York Times* talks about NBC's announcement the day before that it had entered into a long-term agreement with former president Gerald R. Ford under which he would appear in a number of television programs relating to the presidency. The story quotes Herbert S. Schlosser, president of NBC, as saying that Ford agreed with the television network to deliver commentaries on documentaries of programs and that his first appearance would be scheduled for sometime next year. According to the report, Schlosser's statement did not disclose how much the former president would be paid for his appearances on the network's programs, but a spokesman in Ford's transition office in Washington, the story continues, said yesterday that financial details, as well as the number of appearances that Ford would make, were still being worked out. The story says that in another development involving Ford, the Academy for Educational Development, a New York-based nonprofit organization, announced that the former president had been named chairman of its board and would work in Los Angeles for an undisclosed salary. The story points out that the academy, which has an annual income of about $16 million, assists universities and colleges as well as state, local, and foreign governments in solving problems in education and communications. It also focuses on issues related to international affairs. Ford is scheduled to take over as chairman on March 1 from Robert O. Anderson, the oil entrepreneur, the story says.

Analysis: This short news story appeared on the inside page of the *New York Times* and was coded as favorable because it provided Ford the opportunity to share his ideas and feelings about politics generally and the presidency particularly. Although he is officially out of office, this television exposure allowed Ford to continue communicating with Americans to help them understand him better.

March 24, 1977. In this three-column story, which appeared in the inside pages of the *New York Times*, David Bird writes about Gerald R. Ford's warning that "the Soviet Union has embarked on a massive military buildup that threatens the chance for a meaningful arms accord." In what the news story attributes as apparently his strongest foreign policy statement since leaving the U.S. presidency two months before, Ford is quoted as saying that the "historic agreement on strategic arms limitations" reached during his administration was now threatened by the Soviet buildup. According to the story, Ford was speaking before a luncheon given by the Eisenhower Fellowships at the Union Club in New York City, of which he became president last month. In his speech, Ford reportedly gave no details about how the Russians were accelerating the arms race, and no questions were permitted at the luncheon. But in his prepared text, the story points out, Ford said that a warning about the buildup already had been conveyed to the Soviet Union by the narrow margin of the Senate's confirmation of Paul C. Warnke as President Carter's chief arms negotiator. The story says that while in New York, Ford and his wife, Betty, stayed at the new United Nations Plaza Hotel on 44th Street and First Avenue and that the Fords saw the long running Broadway musical, *A Chorus Line.*

Analysis: This is a medium-length news story that was classified as favorable because it helps Ford convey his views on international security to Americans. It also provides an opportunity for him to protest Soviet massive military buildup and to express his fears about how such a buildup portends disaster for the rest of the world. As a statesman, the story helps Ford to reiterate his views on international politics.

May 20, 1977. The story in this day's issue of the *Los Angeles Times* carried the headline: " 'Unmuzzled' Ford Rips Carter Plans." The story begins:

Declaring "I don't intend to be muzzled," former President Gerald R. Ford Thursday night criticized his Democratic successor's economic policies and his proposal for last-minute voter registration.

Inflation has increased by 8% in just 100 days and we have a right to ask why," Ford told a Republican fund-raising dinner.

The story says Ford also attacked President Carter's proposal to permit election-day registration of voters, noting that it was "just too much of an invitation to fraud." Although Ford reportedly criticized the Carter administration, he pledged to "continue to give the new Administration all the support and assistance he could. "But I believe I have the right and obligation to speak out in the national interest," adding, "I am not ready for a rocking chair and I don't intend to be muzzled," the story notes.

Ironically, Ford, who was expected to have a private meeting with President Jimmy Carter during his visit to Washington, the story continues, offered himself as a force for Republican unity, telling GOP partisans that "we have fought each other long enough." The visit was Ford's second to Washington since January, when he left the White House. The story says that Ford began his visit by conferring with GOP congressional leaders. After the meeting, he reportedly said things had not improved substantially since he left office. "I think the public is beginning to see that all the mess in Washington hasn't gotten any better and in some respects it may have deteriorated," he reportedly said, adding, "I have reservations about the performance of the Democratic Congress. I have reservations about some of the programs of the Administration, but I don't intend to be a nitpicker or a sharpshooter." The story states that at the $1,000-a-plate dinner held to raise money for the Senate House GOP Campaign Committee, Ford urged his audience to put less emphasis on ideology and more on attracting independent voters to "the party of common sense." Ford, tanned and healthy-looking, the story points out, also suggested that he might be more critical of Carter and other Democrats in the future.

Analysis: This news story was classified as neutral. While Ford seemed energized and ready to champion the cause of the GOP, he, nonetheless, took some political shots at his successor, who narrowly defeated him in 1976, thus portraying him as being a bit offensive.

May 26, 1977. This news story that appeared in the inside page of the *New York Times* is about former president Gerald R. Ford's asking the legislators of Michigan state to help with funds totaling $3 million to build a museum in his honor in Grand Rapids, where he grew up. Ford is quoted as telling the 16 legislators who met with him over breakfast: "If you could make it possible, I would be deeply grateful. I know what the problems are. I hope you will see your way clear." According to the story, the Michigan House responded favorably later in the afternoon by voting to include $500,000 for the museum in one of its annual appropriations bills. The story says that the legislative leaders indicated that this would probably be the state's "down payment" on its share of the museum. On its part, the story notes, the Michigan Senate did not act, but William Faust, the Senate majority leader, and several other Democrats said that they would support some funding for the museum, but not all that was being sought. Ford reportedly said that the prospects were "excellent" for raising the $6 million needed for the museum and a separate Ford library at the University of Michigan, adding that the state funds would "give me a better argument" in raising money for the project. The story says when one Democrat, Representative Morris Hood Jr. of Detroit, suggested that it would be improper to use public money to honor an active politician because of the possibility of his running for president in 1980, Ford replied that odds were "overwhelmingly" against it, adding that many young bloods were coming up in the Republican Party, "and I don't want anyone preempting the Republican leadership between now and 1980."

Analysis: This news story was classified as short and favorable. It offered the possibility of Ford's realizing his lifetime dream of getting his own museum and library just like the other former U.S. presidents.

December 3, 1977. Richard Bergholz's inside-page story in the *Los Angeles Times* appears under the headline "Ford Assails War Powers Act of 1974." The story says that former president Gerald Ford has observed that when Congress overrode then-president Richard M. Nixon's veto and enacted the War Powers Act in 1974 out of frustration with the Vietnam War, it was a "serious mistake that will come back to haunt us." The story says that Ford told a University of Southern California (USC) international law class that not only was the act an unconstitutional invasion of any president's powers, but it simply was impractical and does not work. In this particular story Ford gave accounts of why he is against the act. He said when the provisions of the act, limiting the right of a president to commit troops overseas and requiring notification and consultation with specified congressional leaders, came into play during the use of U.S. forces to evacuate Americans and others from Da Nang in Vietnam, the following happened:

Congress was in holiday recess and some of the lawmakers who had to be notified of the president's use of U.S. troops were in such faraway places as Mexico, Greece, China and the Middle East.

In another crisis when notification was required, one senator's press aide refused to give the White House the senator's unlisted telephone number, Ford said, and another lawmaker had to be tracked down to a "beach cottage" where local peace officers had to leave a written message on the door, saying "Please call the White House."

Ford reportedly said that those who contended that the curb on the president is necessary to prevent military adventures "simply aren't telling the truth" because, in the Vietnam War and elsewhere, members of Congress had numerous opportunities to cut off funds simply by voting down spending bills. The story says that Ford described as "gutless" the provision of the act that requires the president to withdraw troops after 60 days if Congress has done nothing, suggesting that the members should "have the guts" to approve or disapprove commitment of troops and not hide behind inaction.

Analysis: This story was classified as medium in length. The overall direction or tone of the story was favorable because here Ford was able to articulate forthrightly his views about the War Powers Act, which he strongly believes takes away some of the powers of the American presidency. The story projects a leadership image through the use of rhetoric as he takes on Congress, even though he is officially out of office.

December 20, 1977. Carole Shifrin's news story in the *Washington Post* appears under the headline "Ford Stresses Need for Regulatory Reform." The story says that former president Ford yesterday warned that an opportunity to achieve significant reform of government regulation may be "slipping away," predicting that regulation will probably increase in the years ahead. Speaking at a luncheon held at the American Enterprise Institute conference in Washington, D.C., Ford reportedly complained that various regulatory reform initiatives—some of them begun in his own administration—had yielded "insufficient results." The story says that "while he didn't specifically mention the Carter administration, he pointedly contrasted what he believed to be the national mood when he was leaving office with what he perceives today." Ford then provided four essential elements that he strongly believes will lead to successful reform efforts. The story quoted Ford as making the following suggestions in order for any reform efforts to succeed:

• The administration in power organizing a task force of high-level appointees to tackle the issue on a systematic, continuing basis, with every agency "fully behind the reform effort."
• The President taking a "strong, consistent public stance" on regulatory reform matters....
• Mobilizing a broad coalition drawn from liberal and conservative groups in favor to support the reform movement....
• Addressing a package of reform measures as a unit rather than a piecemeal approach....

This approach, according to Ford, would make it easier for the president to mobilize the public support of reform and more difficult for vested interests to block action.

Analysis: This medium-length, inside-page story, which merely reported Ford's position on regulatory reforms, was classified as favorable. Ford articulated in this report his views about the extent of regulation in America and what needs to be done to ameliorate the situation.

February 19, 1978. James Reston reports in the *New York Times* from Los Angeles about his talk with former president Gerald R. Ford, who was on hand to address a religious Congress of the Laity. Reston notes that Ford "seems more pleased with his life in 'retirement' than he ever did in Congress or in the White House." The reasons for this, Reston explains, include the fact that he was no more "troubled by the economic or metaphysical perplexities of life." Moreover, he is not brooding over his narrow defeat in 1976, and probably no politician of his generation has come out of a quarter of a century in Washington with more friends or fewer enemies, Reston notes. Ford reportedly talked about the past and the future now with more confidence and conviction than ever before. Ford thought that President Carter was in trouble and expected to see him continue to decline in the popularity polls for the rest of that year but said that he takes no pleasure in this. Paradoxically, according to Reston's story, Ford is still fiercely partisan but outspoken in support of President Carter on most foreign policy issues. Ford reportedly said that he was not only backing the administration on the Panama Canal Treaties but defending Carter's decision to send warplanes to Egypt and Saudi Arabia as well as to Israel. The story says that Ford's main criticism of Carter is that "he lost the momentum we had going on the strategic arms negotiations with the Soviet Union, by getting bogged down on side issues," adding, "but maybe, he can get back." Ford insisted that "Congress should be supporting the President more than it is on foreign policy issues," saying: "I understand after Vietnam and Watergate that the Congress wanted to regain some of the power it lost to the White House from the New Deal days on, but it has gone too far. We can't make our way in this kind of a world if the President is weakened by too much Congressional interferences in the conduct of foreign policy."

Analysis: This medium-length, inside-page story was classified as favorable to Ford. Although two paragraphs out of this eight-paragraph story focused on his criticism of Carter, the majority focused on his support of Carter's actions: efforts to move the Panama Canal Treaties initiative and the warplanes deployment to the Middle East. Also, Ford's call on Congress to support the incumbent president, Carter on his foreign policy initiatives, seemed reconciliatory.

April 21, 1978. This story, written by *Los Angeles Times* staff writer Marcida Dodson, talks about how former president Gerald R. Ford has been attending a hospital program on drug and alcohol dependence to gain a better understanding of his wife's current treatment for overmedication. The story says that Ford has been attending seminars and other educational sessions this week at the Long Beach Naval Hospital, where Betty Ford is being treated for dependence on drugs that she takes for acute arthritis, according to Ford's executive assistant Bob Barrett. The former first lady, the story says, was admitted April 11. Barrett was quoted as saying that Ford was attending selected portions of "a basic program that doctors go through." The story quotes Barrett as saying that Ford has attended the program "off and on" this week and would attend his last session today, adding, "Whenever possible, he's been there." According to Barrett, Ford's decision to attend the program grew out of discussions that he had with Mrs. Ford's doctors. The program consists of two weeks of seminars, speeches, and presentations to inform doctors and other military and hospital personnel about alcohol and drug dependence. Barrett reportedly said that Ford was attending for "his general awareness," adding that this could help him assist his wife in her recovery once she returned home.

Analysis: This story was coded as short and was classified as favorable. Generally, it portrayed Ford as a caring, loving husband who understands the urgent need to offer support and encouragement to his wife as she overcomes her overmedication problems.

June 5, 1978. The story in this day's issue of the *New York Times* talks about a speech that Gerald Ford gave at a town meeting in Temple, Texas, regarding whether he would seek the Republican presidential nomination. Ford was quoted as saying that his decision would depend on his assessment of Jimmy Carter's performance over the next year or 18 months. In this story Ford did not hide his feelings, hinting that he was growing deeply disturbed over many of the Carter administration's policies, particularly those that contributed to increased federal spending—and, thus, to inflation. According to the story, the 64-year-old former president, looking tanned, fit, and as though he was enjoying himself hugely, was on his way to Denver through Texas as he undertook yet another leg of the fast-paced tour that will carry him to more than 100 audiences in small towns and big cities between now and the November elections, 157 days away. John M. Crewdson's news story notes that in addition to a speaker's fee of $13,000, Ford's half-hour appearance here was understood to have cost the Temple Chamber of Commerce several thousands in other expenses, ranging from his transportation from California to food for 22 Secret Service agents. The story says that Ford's appearance in Temple was billed as nonpartisan, although he offered his support to Jack Burgess, the Republican candidate for the House seat of W. R. Poage, the area's longtime Democratic congressman, who was retiring soon. According to the story, Ford, at a brief news conference, also took the opportunity to discount recent reports of animosity between himself and President Carter, saying, "I still consider him a friend of mine," but Ford reserved "the right to be critical" of Carter, whom he characterized as having had a "hard time living up to a lot of his campaign promises." The news story also tells of how a recent poll by the Louis Harris organization showed that if a presidential election were held now, Ford would garner 48 percent of the vote to Carter's 43 percent. But, according to the story, Ford dismissed such a survey as "not the basis upon which a person should decide" whether to run for office. Ford is quoted in this report as saying, "There is a lot of time left before I have to make a decision," noting, "At the moment, I'm thoroughly enjoying my retirement."

Analysis: This particular story was classified as medium in length. The overall tone was favorable to Ford, even though he took some political shots at his successor, Jimmy Carter. But most important, the aspect of the story about the Harris poll that gave Ford a slight edge over Carter in the event of a likely presidential election then was particularly positive to Ford.

December 14, 1978. The headline on this *Washington Post* news story reads "Ford Has Wide-Ranging Exchange with Students." It reports of how, since leaving the White House in January 1977, Gerald Ford has become something of an itinerant professor. The *Post*'s staff writer Lawrence Feinberg reports that the former president told 300 students at American University in Washington, D.C., that he has visited 39 colleges in the last 23 months, taught about 270 classes, and answered about 4,000 questions from inquiring students. "I find that the questions are more stimulating, at least to me, than my remarks," Ford reportedly told the students, who laughed appreciatively, and he smiled and laughed, too. Feinberg notes that the questions that followed ranged from Iran, to inflation, to U.S. military strength, and to Ford's plans. According to Feinberg's report, Ford's shortest answer, which was the only one to draw sharp applause, followed a question about former president Nixon's recent statement that he plans to speak about politics again. "I would hope he would stay in the background," Ford is quoted as saying.

The news story says that Ford also spent 45 minutes talking briefly and then answering questions from about 70 law students of the university. Feinberg reports that even though security was tight, with a phalanx of Secret Service agents and a dog sniffing lockers for bombs, the atmosphere of both sessions was lively and informal and that Ford received a warm response. The theme of Ford's speech to the law students, according to the story, was that Congress had encroached too sharply on the power of presidents in both domestic legislation and foreign policy. Ford is quoted as saying: "The pendulum has swung so far that you could almost say we have moved from an imperial presidency to an imperiled presidency. Now we have a Congress that is broadening its powers too greatly." Feinberg writes, "Although most of his comments were nonpartisan, Ford strongly attacked the Carter administration about inflation, which he said now is double the rate it was when he left office." When the question of whether Ford will run for office of president again came up, he reportedly said: "Well, I've been so preoccupied with other things... that I honestly haven't focused on my own future .... All I can say is that I am very healthy and I won't duck any responsibility."

Analysis: This long *Washington Post* news story was coded as favorable. It enabled Ford to share his thoughts and fears about local and global politics and about Nixon, the man whom he pardoned over the shameful Watergate scandal. From the news story, Ford seemed to have enjoyed the students' questions, and they, in turn, appeared to have appreciated his presence.

December 14, 1978. The two-column headline across Robert Shogan's story in this day's issue of the *Los Angeles Times* reads: "Ford Warns of Erosion of Presidential Authority." According to the news story, Gerald R. Ford, who inherited the presidency because of the Watergate abuse of White House power, warned Wednesday that the authority of the presidency is being seriously weakened by Congress and federal regulators. Shogan points out that Ford also had some harsh words for the federal judiciary and its alleged intrusion into governmental and private activities. "The most compelling argument against the judicial activism of recent years is that it tends to subvert democracy itself," Shogan quotes Ford as saying at a luncheon of the American Enterprise Institute, a conservatively oriented research group that made him a "distinguished fellow" when he left the presidency. The story says that Ford, who is believed to harbor hopes of regaining the presidency in 1980, made no mention of his political future. In his speech,

Ford reportedly acknowledged that the Vietnam War and the Watergate scandal had aroused many Americans to the abuse of presidential power. "None of us wants to restore an imperial Presidency," he is quoted as saying, "but neither can we afford an imperiled Presidency." The story says that Ford complained that Congress had recently "gone much too far" in encroaching on prerogatives of the president and the executive branch. Among the specific examples that he cited, according to the story, were attempts to impose a legislative veto over executive actions, the embargo on arms shipments to Turkey, and what he called "continual, day to-day interference" by Congress in the conduct of foreign policy. Because of past abuses, the story notes, Ford charged that the Federal Bureau of Investigation (FBI) and the Central Intelligence Agency (CIA) have been rendered so ineffective "that apparently our best sources of intelligence out of Iran are public newspaper stories." He continued: "There is some feeling in the country today that the Presidents are neither responsible for causing some of our problems nor can they do a great deal about them." The story says that Ford charged that regulatory agencies, such as the Occupational Safety and Health Administration and the Environmental Protection Agency, have resisted Carter's efforts to cut back on government regulation. "We just remind those agencies that they are not, in fact, a separate and distinct fourth branch of the government," he observed in the story. As for the judiciary, Ford reportedly said that it "intrudes into governmental and private institutions and affects the lives of our citizens in ways undreamed of even 25 years ago." He reportedly said that he was opposed to impairing or politicizing the federal judiciary but argued that "wholesale judiciary intervention is not just anti-democratic; it also embroils the courts in problems that are far beyond judicial competence." Ford, the story notes, mentioned specifically the judiciary's taking over administration of prison systems and hospitals and establishing "arbitrary requirements for racial balance" on local school districts.

Analysis: Classified as medium-length, this inside-page news story was coded as favorable to Ford. It shows Ford escalating his attacks on governmental bureaucracy and the need to deregulate the government machinery to make the pieces work more efficiently.

October 20, 1979. This *Washington Post* story written by Mary Russell ends speculations about Gerald Ford's intention to run for the 1980 Republican presidential nomination. The report says that Ford has eliminated himself as an "active" candidate for the nomination and that he has urged his supporters to work for other candidates. "I urge those who may have held back to ascertain my intentions, to jump into the fray in behalf of the candidate of their choice," Ford is quoted as saying in a statement released to journalists. The story notes that Ford has repeatedly said that he is not a candidate for the nomination and did not expect to become one, but yesterday's statement, made to reporters in the House press gallery in Washington, D.C., went further than those past statements. Ford was said to have characterized the statement as more "definitive" than others. According to the story, Ford said that he had made a "firm decision not to become an active candidate," adding that he would not permit anyone else to enter his name in a primary or state contest. The story says that Ford did not close the door on a draft but admitted that the likelihood of a "brokered convention is very remote." He is quoted as saying: "I would reconsider my position only if my party felt it was essential for me to do so or if unforeseen circumstances developed." But when asked what those circumstances might be, according to the story, Ford said, "I don't know. You define it." The story explains that Ford associates believe that it would take the unexpected collapse of Ronald Reagan's campaign to bring him into the race and that Ford denied that he was pressured into the decision by other Republican leaders, maintaining, "This was totally done by myself." Asked if his wife, Betty, had pressured him not to run, Ford reportedly said, "Betty and I have always had a working relationship," but he added that it was basically his decision.

Analysis: This news story, coded as short, was classified as favorable because it laid to rest all speculations about Ford's running for the U.S. presidency again. It no doubt elevated his standing among his admirers as an honorable and well-principled man who takes pride in his present status as an elder statesman and would therefore not jeopardize that role for any public office.

CARTER'S PORTRAYAL IN THE PRESS

January 24, 1981. This inside-page story in the *New York Times* announced that former president Jimmy Carter and his wife, Rosalynn, would fly Tuesday to the U.S. Virgin Islands to begin a vacation of two to three weeks. The announcement, attributed to an unnamed Carter family spokesman, says that the Carters delayed their vacation until a week after the president left office, allowing him to travel to West Germany to greet the American hostages who had been in Iran. The delay was also to give the Carters' daughter, Amy, time to enroll in her new school near Plains, Georgia.

Analysis: This very short news item was classified as neutral because there was not enough information to really establish a tone.

January 24, 1981. This *Washington Post* feature article written by George Lardner Jr. talks about former president Jimmy Carter's takeover of his presidential papers. The story appeared under the headline "Records of the Carter Presidency Trucked on Down to Georgia." Lardner begins by recounting how shortly after the November 1980 elections, the archivist of the United States sent a note to high-ranking officials of about 50 federal agencies, reminding them of the law concerning government records. Lardner says that the official note reminded employees of "the criminal penalties that are attached to unlawful removal or destruction of federal records." According to Lardner, the rules emphasized that the definition of official records involves materials made or received either under federal law or in connection with the transaction of public business. Official records are public records and belong to the office rather than to the officer, Lardner notes.

But, according to Lardner, Carter did not see it quite that way, at least as far as the records of his four years at the White House were concerned. The feature article notes that millions of documents have just been trucked to Georgia under the traditional theory that they are all Carter's personal property. The records include staffers' telephone logs, appointment books, office diaries, and personal notes on all sorts of subjects involving government business. According to the article, the boxes containing the documents were carted off to Andrew Air Force Base to join a 19-truck caravan for the trip to Atlanta Tuesday morning. It says that the records, estimated by James E. O'Neill, assistant archivist for presidential libraries, as covering possibly 30 million pages, would be processed and stored in an old post office annex in downtown Atlanta until a Carter library can be built. The article observes that the convoy to Georgia, under military guard to protect all the top-secret documents affecting national security that Carter is taking with him, marked the end of an era. It explains that under a law enacted in 1978, all presidential papers, from Ronald Reagan's on, will belong to the government and eventually will be subject to public scrutiny under uniform standards fixed by statue. The article notes that what is surprising about the passing of the era, however, is the vigor with which the outgoing president, Carter, is asserting private custody and control of records that, in signing the 1978 law, he has acknowledged should in general be public property. Lardner quotes former White House deputy counsel Michael Cardozo as bristling at the notion that Carter was continuing a double standard for presidential papers as distinct from other government records. Cardozo reportedly said that there was a solid tradition of personal ownership for presidential papers, going back to George Washington.

Analysis: This medium-length feature article in the inside page of the *Post* was classified as neutral. It discusses the pros and cons of Carter's acquisition of his presidential records for display in his own presidential library later to be built in Atlanta, Georgia.

January 27, 1981. A week after Jimmy Carter left office, the *Washington Post* carried several letters from its readers under the general headline "Exit Jimmy Carter," in which they express their views and perceptions of his administration. One writer says: "Frankly, I was glad when Jimmy Carter was elected in 1976.... Despite some setbacks, I don't think Mr. Carter was a failure. I'll never regret having voted for him." Another says that perhaps the best thing that can be said about Carter's presidency is that it brought the American people to their senses because after more than a decade of moral decline and cultural decay, "we needed a weak and feeble president to make us painfully aware of how weak and feeble we've been." One other writer talks about Carter's final budget message to Congress, which contains, for example, replacing "the present 4 cents-a-gallon federal tax on gasoline and diesel fuels with a 14-cents-per-gallon tax effective June 1.... Sort of going away present. Remember him kindly," the letter concludes. In yet another letter, a writer lists Carter's accomplishments—which include the Camp David accords, the Panama Canal treaties, the human rights policy, reopening diplomatic relations with China, civil service reform, and active use of the vice president, as well as widespread appointment of minority judges and officials—noting that, "It may be a long time before a president of such authentic character holds office." In yet another letter, the writer recalls Carter's farewell speech of January 14 and notes that "we were correct in denying him a second term," adding: "The sense of despair, hopelessness and impending destruction that he projected was characteristic of his approach to governing the country. I had hoped that his overwhelming defeat would have indicated to him that the American people believe that the future may be promising and productive." Furthermore, another expresses deep respect for Carter for "exercising patience, courage, faith and commitment to peace in solving the hostage crisis," adding: "This is the first modern crisis of major proportion to be solved in the world without war." Still another writer characterizes Carter as "a good man, an honest man, and a noble man," saying, "Although his intelligence was unquestioned, his use of it was." The writer says Carter "believed too much in the goodness of people that he could not bring himself to undertake any action that would end the evil threatening all he held dear. Ultimately, it was his unwillingness to act that brought about his tragedy."

Analysis: The collection of letters was coded as long because it occupied a considerable portion of the letters page. The collection was classified as neutral because it provided a divided, well-balanced view of how Americans perceive Carter and his administration. The *Post* treated these letters as one collection with a general headline, and so was the author's analysis.

March 7, 1981. This inside-page story in the *New York Times* announces that former president Jimmy Carter is to be the eighth recipient of the Harry S Truman Public Service Award. The announcement was made by Mayor E. Lee Corner of Independence, Missouri, Truman's hometown. The story explains that Carter was chosen for the honor primarily because in the final days of his tenure, he worked quietly but persistently for the freedom of the 52 American hostages held in Tehran. "Although his efforts have gone almost unheralded, he exhibited exceedingly strong dedication to the task of a peaceful release," Corner is quoted as saying. The story says that Carter is to receive the public service award, a copy of a bronze statue of Truman, in Independence Square on May 8, Truman's birthday. Previous recipients of the Truman award include Clark Clifford, Hubert H. Humphrey, Stuart Symington, Leon Jaworski, and Henry A. Kissinger.

Analysis: This short news story was classified as favorable because it announces yet another distinguished award for Jimmy Carter.

August 25, 1981. This story in the *Washington Post* announces former president Jimmy Carter's arrival in Peking tonight for a visit in which he would receive red-carpet treatment from Chinese leaders, grateful for his role in normalizing U.S.–China relations. Calling the trip "a wonderful occasion for us," the story says that Carter led his wife, Rosalynn, and daughter, Amy, off the plane to be greeted by Chinese officials headed by Vice Foreign Minister Zhang Wenjin. According to the story, Carter asked after the health of Chinese Communist Party vice chairman Deng Xiaoping, who presided over the delicate negotiations leading to the historic 1978 accord in which the two former adversaries normalized their relations. The story says that Carter was told that Deng was well and looking forward to meeting him. Carter, the story notes, would also meet Premier Zhao Ziyang, who would give a banquet in his honor Tuesday night. Carter, who was presented with bouquets of flowers on arrival, described Deng's visit to the United States in 1979 as "one of the most exciting we had." According to the story, had he not been defeated by Ronald Reagan, Carter had been expected to come to China this year on a state visit. But tonight, the story points out, it almost looked as if Carter was still in office, judging from the actions of the Chinese, who are noted for not forgetting their friends.

Analysis: This inside-page story was classified as medium-length and favorable. It not only announced Carter's red-carpet treatment visit to China but also talked about how happy the Chinese were in welcoming him to their country.

August, 26, 1981. "Carter Reminds Reagan of One-China Commitment" screams the headline on Michael Parks' inside story in this day's *Los Angeles Times.* The story reads:

PEKING—Former President Jimmy Carter, who established full diplomatic relations with Peking, reminded the Reagan Administration on Tuesday that further development of the strategically important partnership requires strict American observance of the agreement recognizing the Communist government and Taiwan as part of China.

Carter, speaking at a banquet in his honor at the start of a 10-day visit to China, his first major appearance since leaving the White House, said he believes that the improvement in Sino-American relations is irreversible. But he clearly shared some of Peking's concern that President Reagan might restore U.S. diplomatic recognition of Chinese Nationalist regime on Taiwan and thereby jeopardize the new alliance with Peking.

"The Sino-American relationship already has contributed significantly to the solving of (international) problems," Carter said, citing "expansionism, pressure on natural resources and the worldwide threat to peace."

"With continuing adherence by both sides to the principles of the normalization agreement, its potential is even greater," he said.

Carter told Premier Zhao Ziyang that he tried in late 1978, when the two countries agreed on full relations, to give those new ties sufficient strength that "progress would be so rapid and of such obvious value that it would be irreversible and able to withstand the inevitable shocks of changing political times." This has happened, he declared.

Zhao underscored Peking's continuing concern that the agreement establishing diplomatic relations be fully honored, but he indicated general satisfaction with the assurances that China has recently received from the Reagan Administration.

"Attaching importance to the strategic significance of the relations between China and the United States," Zhao said, "President Reagan has expressed his readiness to continue to strengthen the friendly ties and cooperation between the two countries on the basis of the communique on the establishment of diplomatic relations." That communique was issued on Dec. 15, 1978. Ambassadors were in place the following March.

This news story says that Zhao praised Carter as an American statesman well known to Chinese people, adding, "You made great contributions to Sino-American relations."

Analysis: This news story was classified not only as long but as favorable to Carter. It not only got Carter a hero's welcome but also boosted his image among Chinese leaders in the process.

January 7, 1982. Charles Mohr writes in this issue of the *New York Times* about Jimmy Carter's published article on fly-fishing in the *Fly Fisherman* magazine of January/February 1982. In his seven-page article called "Spruce Creek Diary" Carter describes a weeklong vacation taken last May by his entire family on the same central Pennsylvania limestone stream that he sometimes fished, in seclusion, while in office. Mohr's story notes that almost all modern presidents have been fishermen of sorts, although many have favored trolling lures from the comfortable chairs of cabin cruisers. However, Carter, Mohr notes, is the first serious fly fisherman since Dwight D. Eisenhower and Herbert Hoover, who wrote a book about his own days in pursuit of trout called *Fishing for Fun.*

Analysis: The above short story was classified as favorable because it provided Carter the opportunity to showcase his lifetime outdoor adventures and favorite pastimes, which include fishing.

May 2, 1982. The headline on this *Washington Post* story was straight to the point: "Carter Blames Reagan for 'Hardships.' " Michel McQueen and Martin Weil, whose bylines appear over the story, writes from Silver Spring in the Washington, D.C. metropolitan area:

Former president Jimmy Carter asserted here last night that "ill-advised" Reagan administration actions have brought millions of Americans economic hardship unknown since the Great Depression, and called on his party to offer a positive program in what he said "will be a good Democratic year."

Carter, speaking at a party fund-raising dinner in only his third visit here since surrendering the White House, told an enthusiastic audience of 1,300 that while he is no longer interested in public office, "people will recognize that they made a serious mistake in 1980" when they chose Ronald Reagan as president.

The story notes that Carter called on Democrats to shun confrontation and "negative, divisive political attacks." But rather than partisan rhetoric, the story points out, Carter said "what the country wants to see is a country bound together." This *Post* story says that Carter, who has been relatively silent on political issues since leaving office, appeared yesterday largely to be heeding his own advice to mute divisive rhetoric. Rather than attacking the Reagan administration policies, Carter chose to express what he said were the concerns of American people. According to the story, Carter also spoke about an impending trip abroad where he plans to speak at town hall-style meetings in foreign capitals, and about his upcoming memoirs, on which he has been working in Georgia since he left Washington.

Analysis: This is a long news item that was classified as favorable because it casts Carter in a better light—as someone who can still pull together large crowds.

October 11, 1982. This news item, written by Doyle McManus and headlined, "Carter Says U.S. Agents Infiltrated Iran," appeared in the inside pages of the *Los Angeles Times*. According to the story, former president Jimmy Carter disclosed in excerpts from his memoirs that American secret agents operated in Iran easily and repeatedly during the 14-month crisis over the seizure of U.S. Embassy and hostages in Tehran. McManus quotes him as saying that "Our agents... moved freely in and out of Tehran under the guise of business or media missions." Carter reportedly cited two specific missions undertaken by the "clandestine operatives preparing for the abortive commando mission to rescue the hostages, and helping the Canadian Embassy in Tehran smuggle out six American diplomats who had taken refuge there." According to McManus, excerpts from Carter's memoirs published by the *Time* magazine did not provide details of the agents' activities or their false identities as businessmen and journalists. Carter points out in his book that the rescue mission, which collapsed April 24, 1980, when three of eight helicopters failed, was preceded by intense intelligence-gathering. He is quoted as writing: "... we received information from someone (who cannot be identified) who was thoroughly familiar with the compound, knew where every hostage was located, how many and what kind of guards were there at different times and the daily schedule of the hostages and their captors." McManus writes that although Carter did not identify the informant, *Newsweek* magazine reported last July that the embassy's Pakistani cook furnished the Central Intelligence Agency (CIA) with those details of the hostages' locations. McManus concludes his story by saying that Carter observed in his memoir that if the rescue mission had succeeded, or if some other way had been found to release the hostages before the 1980 presidential election, his reelection "would have been assured," and he would still be in the White House today.

Analysis: This story was classified as medium in length. Because it focused solely on the ill-fated American hostage rescue attempt in Tehran, it brings back memories of this sad event in American history, which ultimately cost Carter a second term in office. Without a doubt it was unfavorable to the image of Jimmy Carter.

March 11, 1983. The two-column headline on this inside-page story in the *Los Angeles Times* reads: "Carter Visits Gaza; New W. Bank Protests Erupt." Basically, this story reports how Jimmy Carter went to the Gaza Strip in the Middle East under heavy Israeli army guard Thursday to meet a leading Palestinian and how West Bank Arabs staged demonstrations to protest his trip to Israel. The story quotes Israeli radio as saying that there were no incidents in the Gaza Strip when Carter visited Rashid Shawa, who was mayor of Gaza City until the Israelis ousted him last year for refusal to cooperate with Israel. But in the West Bank, the story continues, three Israelis were injured by rocks thrown in demonstrations. The story says that the radio reported that in one incident, Israeli motorists fired weapons at stone-throwing demonstrators but caused no casualties. The story quoted a police spokesman as saying that Arab youths pelted passing vehicles with rocks in Arab East Jerusalem, and the military said that in Ramallah, six miles north of the Israeli capital, soldiers dispersed a Palestinian crowd that threw pieces of metal at them. According to the story, Palestinians of the West Bank and Gaza complained that the 1978 Camp David accords worked out during the Carter administration ignored their rights. The story points out that Carter had closed-door meetings with residents of Gaza to discuss problems in the region. According to the story, Carter refused to answer questions but expressed the belief that Israel and the Palestinians should negotiate. He did not suggest a role for the Palestine Liberation Organization, however, the story says. Later in the day, the story notes, Carter, citing the success of direct negotiations at Camp David, called for Israel and the Palestinians to conduct face-to-face talks to achieve "comprehensive peace with justice."

Analysis: Classified as medium-length and neutral, this news story depicts how volatile and delicate the question of peace and stability is in the Middle East.

July 14, 1983. The Home section of this day's issue of the *New York Times* featured the log cabin of Jimmy and Rosalynn Carter, located deep in the Blue Ridge Mountains of northwest Georgia. This long article, written by Enid Nemy, shows photographs of the Carters enjoying and relaxing in their second home as well as some of the furniture in the cabin. Nemy sets the tone:

The sun filters in through groves of towering white oak and hemlock, and the sound of water is constant as it trickles over the rocks of Turnip Town Creek from a small waterfall and continues for seven or eight miles to the Ellijay River.

It is an idyllic setting, deep in the Blue Ridge Mountains of northwest Georgia, cozily close to the Tennessee border. The log cabin, perched alongside the creek, is remote from the main highway, reached by a long winding, tricky and not particularly good gravel road. The cabin might almost be removed from civilization but for the small building that guards the entrance and the men who appear the moment a vehicle is heard. For this is the second home, the hideaway, of Jimmy and Rosalynn Carter, and for a former President and First Lady, privacy does not preclude the Secret Service.

According to Nemy, this is the first season that the Carters have used the cabin, built last year by John Pope, who is in the construction business, and whose wife, Betty, is a cousin of the former president. The design, though basically from a kit, includes an amalgam of details added by the two couples. Nemy points out that the Carters and the Popes are joint owners of the 10-acre plot and the cabin, although the Popes live in another house just a neighborly drive away at the top of Walnut Mountain. The cabin, whose exterior is made of hand-hewn yellow pine logs from the surrounding area, is a 30-foot square, divided into three rooms and two bathrooms on two floors. The interior floors and walls are also pine, with the walls alternating between smooth-finished wood and hand sewn logs. According to Nemy, almost all the furniture—tables, chairs, stools, deacon's bench, armoires, and beds—was made by Carter at his workshop in Plains, and much of it is his design. The hickory and the pine used for the furniture also came from Plains, the hickory chopped from a grove behind the Carter residence there. The pine, dating from 1833, came from the house where Mrs. Carter was born, which was built by her great-great-grandfather. Nemy talks about how when Carter is not on the porch, reading or weaving bark seats for the chairs that he makes, he is likely to be in the creek, building a dam or fishing for trout, with his Willie Nelson or Levi jeans covered by thigh-high, waterproof boots.

Analysis: This long feature article about the Carters' log cabin perched inside the deep woods of the Blue Ridge Mountains of Georgia was classified as favorable. It provides the reader a glimpse of the former first family's vacation home, their taste in furniture and decor, and how they are now living as private citizens outside the White House.

August 7, 1983. This story, published in the *Washington Post*, was excerpted from an interview with Jimmy Carter in the *Christian Science Monitor* of August 4. The question was: "Is the president taking great risks in Central America?" Carter replied that he thinks President Reagan was taking great risks. He said military escalation always is risky. Carter wondered whether the democratic nations' closing all doors to the Sandinistas gave them no alternative but to turn to Havana and Moscow. According to Carter, when the Sandinistas took over, he was disturbed by some of their policies, adding that he thought they were too far to the left. "There were some human rights abuses under them," Carter said, "but we tried to give them some economic aid." The former president recalled how he met with the junta members in the Oval Office, went over his own grievances on what they were doing, urged them to initiate reforms, and predicated economic aid on those reforms being carried out. "I minimized the military approach," Carter said, adding:

I don't know, at this point, how much willingness there is for negotiations. My judgment is that the Contadora group and the Nicaraguans want to negotiate. My judgment is that the Reagan administration, including [U.N. Ambassador Jeane J.] Kirkpatrick, are opposed to negotiation. I don't know about the Hondurans. The Hondurans obviously have a duality of authority.... I don't really know under what circumstance the Honduran military forces or the government leaders are willing to negotiate.

Carter also said in the interview that he had little doubt that if President Reagan joined with the Contadoran leaders and demanded that the Hondurans negotiate under the auspices of the Organization of American States (OAS), the Hondurans would certainly succumb to that request.

Analysis: This interview excerpt was classified as short and favorable to Carter. It highlights Carter's concerns in Central America and his White House efforts in initiating political and economic reforms in the region.

PORTRAYAL OF REAGAN IN THE PRESS

January 26, 1989. The story in this issue of the *New York Times* talks about Simon & Schuster's announcement that it would publish Ronald Reagan's memoirs and a collection of speeches selected by the former president. The writer, Edwin McDowell, quotes Richard E. Snyder, chairman and chief executive officer of Simon & Schuster, as saying that "few presidents have influenced mainstream America the way Ronald Reagan has," adding, "Without question, President Reagan's memoirs will become one of the most valuable historical documents of this century, and we're proud to have been chosen as his publisher." According to this story, no one involved in the negotiations would disclose the financial terms of the contract, by which Simon & Schuster acquired world rights, but it was thought likely to have totaled several million dollars. The story says that yesterday's announcement surprised publishing industry officials because Reagan was not thought to have been interested in writing his memoirs. The story quotes the publisher as saying that the memoir would consist of personal reminiscences as well as reflections on Reagan's life and achievements and on key events, successes, and disappointments of his years in office.

Analysis: Coded as short and classified as favorable, this piece of news raises expectations among Reagan's friends and admirers who would love to read his memoirs and about his presidency.

October 26, 1989. This *Washington Post* story written from Tokyo by Elisabeth Bumiller says that former president Ronald Reagan today defended Japan's purchases of American companies and real estate and spoke in favor of Sony Corp.'s recent buyout of Columbia Pictures. Reagan reportedly made his remarks in a taped interview broadcast by Fuji Television, the national network of Fujisankei Communications Group, a media conglomerate that reportedly is paying the former president $2 million for the visit. Bumiller reports that when asked about Sony's purchase of Columbia Pictures Entertainment Corp. for $3.4 billion last month, Reagan responded, "I don't think there's anything wrong with that." He added, "Probably we might see some improvements... [because] I'm not too proud of Hollywood these days with the immorality that is shown in pictures, and the vulgarity. I just have a feeling that maybe Hollywood needs some outsiders to bring back decency and good taste to some of the pictures that are being made." Again, when asked about Japanese investment in the United States, Reagan reportedly said: "The United States still is the widest investor in other countries, owning properties that are an investment and so forth, so how can we complain if someone wants to invest in us? As a matter of fact, I think they want to invest in us because we're a good investment." This news report also talks about how "very proud and pleased" Reagan said that he was about the student-led movement for democracy in China; but stopped short of full endorsement of the pro-democracy protesters. This report notes that later at a banquet sponsored by Fujisankei, Reagan called on Japan to send economic aid to Poland in support of that country's bid for democracy.

Analysis: This long story, appearing in the inside pages of the *Washington Post*, was classified as neutral. Although Reagan appeared to be in control, expressing his opinions about the American entertainment industry, he seemed a bit awkward and inconsistent in his position as a former head of the Screen Actors Guild. No doubt his utterances later came back to haunt him as he was forced to apologize to Hollywood for asking the industry to look to Japan to bring back decency to American films and movies.

February 1, 1990. "Ban on False Endorsements Pushed" reads the headline over this news item in this day's issue of the *Los Angeles Times*. The story, written by staff writer Ralph Frammolino, notes that Reagan has endorsed legislation introduced Wednesday aimed at closing a legal loophole that allegedly enabled an Orange County legislator to forge Reagan's signature on campaign materials without facing criminal penalties. The story says that the legislation was introduced in reaction to a recent court decision dismissing felony forgery charges against Assemblyman John R. Lewis (R-Orange) for using the unauthorized Reagan signature on 480,000 campaign letters in 1986. The story points out that the 3rd District Court of Appeals held last week that Lewis' use of the phony Reagan signatures did not defraud the voters of money or property—ingredients needed to warrant a criminal charge. The story says Attorney General John K. Van de Kamp, who helped draft the new bill, said Wednesday that he will appeal the ruling to the state Supreme Court. According to the story, the appeals court decision stunned many legislators, who said that they were afraid that it will encourage unscrupulous campaigners to forge signatures of well-known politicians and celebrities without fear of sanction. The story recalled a press conference called by Senator William A. Craven (R-Oceanside) in which he announced the introduction of a bill to make forging someone's name on campaign material a crime that could result in three years in prison and a $50,000 fine. The story notes that Reagan spokesman Mark Weinberg said: "President Reagan supports Sen. Craven's bipartisan bill because it seeks to protect the good name, personal signature and political speech of every citizen. The right to publicly endorse or oppose candidates or initiatives is as precious as the right to vote on them."

Analysis: This news story was classified as medium-length and favorable. In this story Reagan threw his weight behind supporters fighting to make it a criminal offense for people to forge signatures that may likely be used to influence the outcome of democratic elections.

February 10, 1990. This news story carried in the *Los Angeles Times* discusses how former president Ronald Reagan would forgo his right to executive privilege in order to testify on videotape as a defense witness in John M. Poindexter's Iran–Contra trial. According to *Times* staff writer Norman Kempster, Reagan would be questioned under oath by Poindexter's lawyers and cross-examined by the Iran–Contra special counsel during the taping. Kempster's story notes that although Reagan previously provided information about the scandal that broke during his second term, the videotaped testimony would be the closest that he has come to the give-and-take of a court of law. According to the story, in a four-page brief filed with U.S. district judge Harold Greene, Reagan lawyers said that the use of video-tape—instead of live testimony in the courtroom—would permit the former president to respond to questions without running the risk of inadvertently disclosing sensitive national secrets. If such secrets were mentioned, they would be deleted from the tape, the lawyers argued. The brief said that Reagan "recognizes that the videotape deposition format will provide an appropriate mechanism for all parties, including the incumbent and former presidents, to protect sensitive, classified national security information and confidential deliberations." The story notes that Reagan's attorney, Theodore B. Olson, said that the former president "will not assert executive privilege" with respect to the videotaped testimony. He added that Reagan would defer to President Bush and the Justice Department "with respect to issues of executive privilege concerning national security or foreign affairs that may arise during the taking of the videotaped deposition." In an earlier order, the story points out, Greene said that he would preside over the former president's testimony, ruling on objections raised by lawyers from either side. Specifically, the judge was reported as saying that he would consider claims of executive privilege or national security that might be raised as the taping goes along. Providing background to the case, the story recalls that in contrast to his agreement to give oral testimony, Reagan earlier this week invoked executive privilege in an effort to avoid turning over to Poindexter's lawyers more than 30 excerpts from his White House diaries. Greene has said that he would hold a hearing to determine whether Reagan's claim of constitutionally guaranteed confidentiality outweighs Poindexter's need for evidence to defend himself.

Analysis: This long news story appearing in the inside pages of the *Los Angeles Times* was classified as neutral. The arguments for and against the videotaped deposition were well balanced and never overwhelmingly favored one party over the other.

April 13, 1990. Staff writer Patt Morrison writes in this day's issue of the *Los Angeles Times* that a nine-and-half-foot-high, 6,338-pound chunk of the Berlin Wall was unveiled at the Reagan Library in Simi Valley, California. The story begins: Folks, you may have caught the act during its long-running engagement, 28 years in Berlin, and now it's here, in Ventura County. Ladies and gentlemen, let's say "Ich bin ein Venturer," and give a big Simi Valley welcome to a big performer; the concrete you love to hate—the Berlin Wall!

The story reports of the pomp and circumstance that marked this "sunny outdoor ceremony that blended patriotism and razzmatazz—a German oompah band direct from San Diego and Mel Torme's singing the national anthem—" and where the workmen wore caps that read "Building One for the Gipper." The story recalls how not quite three years ago Reagan visited West Berlin and, in front of the Brandenburg Gate, demanded: "Mr. Gorbachev, tear down this wall." The story quotes Reagan as saying that the wall "shattered dreams and crushed hopes. It made us angry.... Let our children and grandchildren come here and see this wall and reflect on what it meant to history. Let them understand that only vigilance and strength will deter tyranny."

Analysis: This story was classified as short and favorable. Without a doubt it casts Reagan in a favorable light as the man who helped destroy the Iron Curtain, which literally divided the world into West and East blocs for a very long time. Here Reagan finally gets to display a piece of the infamous Berlin Wall in his presidential library, capping off his sustained and systematic efforts in ending Communism as we know it.

September 18, 1990. This news story written by *Los Angeles Times* staff writer John-Thor Dahlburg reports that Ronald Reagan returned to Moscow to a bear-hug welcome from Soviet president Mikhail S. Gorbachev. Reagan is reported to have said that so much has changed since his last visit that he feels like Rip Van Winkle, the man in a tale who slept for 20 years and woke to find a far different world. The visit, according to the news report, was Reagan's first to the Soviet Union since his Moscow summit meeting with Gorbachev in May 1988, when he strolled on Red Square and said that this country could no longer be considered an "evil empire," as he had labeled it five years earlier. Reagan, who was accompanied by his wife, Nancy, was in Moscow on the invitation of Gorbachev. Dahlburg reports that Reagan marveled at the improved state of U.S.–Soviet relations and gave himself and his host some of the credit for moving the superpowers away from mistrust to "cautious friendship." Reagan was quoted as telling journalists: "I think, frankly, [that] President Gorbachev and I discovered a sort of a bond between all the people."

Dahlburg says the former U.S. president and his Soviet host, both beaming and visibly delighted to be in each other's company again, embraced heartily as they met for private talks in Gorbachev's office at the Kremlin. Gorbachev, Dahlburg notes, apologized to Reagan for Moscow's drizzly and overcast weather, saying that he supposed it was hotter in Los Angeles and San Francisco, the city where he and his wife, Raisa, last met with the Reagans after the June superpower summit in Washington. The report quotes the Soviet official news agency, Tass, as saying that Gorbachev told Reagan that he believes that significant results can be reached "in the foreseeable future" in U.S.–Soviet talks on cutting their strategic nuclear arsenals by half. The report says that Reagan, who also spoke to the International Affairs Committee of the Supreme Soviet, or national legislature, was stunned by the numerous changes that have taken place in the Soviet Union since he last saw the country. He likened the dramatically increased striving for independence and sovereignty by individual Soviet republics to the rancorous disputes that led to the U.S. Civil War. According to Dahlburg, Reagan took the opportunity to lecture the Soviet lawmakers on the benefits of capitalism, explaining in the elementary terms of an Economics 101 textbook what *supply-and-demand economy* is all about (emphasis added).

Analysis: This story, in the inside page of the *Washington Post*, was classified as favorable. It shows both Reagan and Gorbachev celebrating their friendship and the camaraderie that melted the cold walls of suspicion and distrust between the United States and the Soviet Union several years ago. It also shows the human side of the two leaders and their vision for a united, safe world.

November 4, 1990. This article, which examines former president Ronald Reagan's memoir, titled *An American Life*, appeared in the Book Review section of the *Los Angeles Times*. The reviewer, Richard Reeves, says that Reagan "proved to be an extraordinarily effective leader, for better or worse," noting, "Presidents are not paid by the hour. They are paid for their judgement, remembered only for the big ones, three or four big decisions, often reactive." According to Reeves, Reagan came to office with an agenda, and he pushed it with all his considerable might, changing America at least for a time—a time that continues, for better or worse. American attitudes, under his leadership and example, shifted from "We're all in this together," to "You're on your own, buddy; don't tell me your troubles." Reeves notes that *An American Life* is American to the point of fantasy, and it also is surprisingly defensive, with the author's blaming Congress, the press, or his own staff for anything big or small that seemed to go wrong on his watch—as if words now can change what he did then. Reeves quotes Reagan as saying: "I hope history will look back on the eighties, not only as a period of economic recovery and a time when we put the brakes on the growth of government, but as a time for fundamental change for our economy and a resurgence of the American spirit of generosity that touched off an unprecedented outpouring of good deeds." Reeves notes that the Reagan deeds—good or bad is in the eyes of the beholder—to be remembered, at least in the short term, are the fact that he restructured the American economy, using tax cuts and deregulation to favor what his vice president and successor, George Bush, called the "investing classes." Reagan, Reeves points out, more than doubled the size and power of the U.S. military, claiming that the buildup—"Peace through Strength"—was the final demonstration to Soviet leaders that they could never defeat the United States militarily or economically, a buildup leading to the dramatic end of 45 years of nuclear-dangerous Cold War. Also, Reeves writes: "Reagan tried to dismantle much of the incomplete American welfare state, but ended up replacing the liberal politics of 'tax and spend' with a destructive conservative policy of 'spend and borrow'—leaving his successors and his people with horrendous debts and deficits in the Federal budget and America's trade balance." According to Reeves, there is noting new in the book, with the exception of long excerpts from extensive, sometimes weekly correspondence between Reagan and Soviet president Mikhail Gorbachev over arms-control agreements. Reeves says that Reagan does not open up very much in his memoirs, offering bewildered or bewildering accounts of such things as the plots and crimes of Iran–Contra and a series of charming stories, like the one about Prince Charles of England's asking for tea at the White House but not drinking any because he did not know what to do with a tea bag—apparently he had never seen one before.

Analysis: This long book review was classified as neutral because it was well balanced. As the reviewer puts it, Reagan's deeds, good or bad, are in the eyes of the beholder.

February 7, 1991. This article in the *Washington Post* written by Lou Cannon, profiles former president Ronald Reagan on the occasion of his 80th birthday. Cannon writes about a ceremony at Beverly Hills, California, in honor of Reagan that was attended by several dignitaries and entertainers, including former British prime minister and "special friend" Margaret Thatcher. The article says that video-taped greetings were sent by President George Bush, Canadian prime minister Brian Mulroney, and Polish president Lech Walesa. Reagan also received congratulatory phone calls from several national and world figures, including former president Richard Nixon, former Joint Chiefs of Staff chairman Colin Powell, Secretary of State James Baker, German chancellor Helmut Kohl, and South Korean president Roh Tae Woo. According to Cannon, the ceremony was conducted in an atmosphere of patriotic fervor marked by the playing of a San Diego Marine Corps band and a rendition of "God Bless the U.S.A," which became a Republican anthem during the 1984 campaign, led by the songs of Lee Greenwood. Reagan reportedly used the occasion to reminisce on his life, from the small towns of central Illinois, to careers as a sports announcer and movie actor, and, finally, to the highest office in the land. Reagan reportedly said that his earlier acting career had been crucial to his ability to perform as president. Cannon narrates that Reagan, blowing out eight candles on a four-tiered cake and getting some of the icing on his tuxedo, wished that "God will watch over each and every one of our men and women who are bravely serving in the Persian Gulf—and their families, wherever they may be—and may they know that we as a nation stand firmly behind them." Paying tribute to Reagan as the featured speaker for the evening, Cannon quotes Thatcher as saying that Reagan's "abiding" contribution was that he "set out to enlarge freedom the world over when freedom was in retreat," adding, while looking toward Reagan, "and you succeeded—with perhaps a little help from friends." Cannon notes that the evening ended on an emotional note with Reagan and wife, Nancy, leading nearly 1,000 guests in singing "God Bless America."

Analysis: This long story, which appeared in the Style section of the *Post*, was extremely favorable to Ronald Reagan. It portrayed Reagan as a man with many committed friends and admirers who recognize his contributions to democracy and freedom throughout the world.

March 29, 1991. This editorial in the *New York Times*, headlined "Mr. Reagan Finally Leads on Guns," applauds Ronald Reagan for finally supporting James Brady for gun control legislation. The full text is reprinted:

The gun control campaign conducted by James Brady, who was wounded in the 1981 Presidential assassination attempt, has touched millions of Americans. But until yesterday, one prominent American remained oddly silent. Ronald Reagan, target of the bullet Mr. Brady stopped, seemed oblivious to his former press secretary's cause.

In a speech yesterday and an article on today's Op-Ed page, Mr. Reagan finally breaks his silence with a resounding endorsement of the so-called Brady bill. His welcome support adds heft to growing pressure for the bill and puts President Bush, who continues to oppose it, on the spot.

The bill, introduced by Representative Edward Feighan, Democrat of Ohio, would impose a national seven-day waiting period between purchase and delivery of a handgun so police could check the purchaser's background. Similar laws in several states, including Mr. Reagan's native California, block thousands of illegal gun sales each year.

The National Rifle Association resists the national bill and argues that few criminals go to gun shops to purchase guns. That's true—but beside the point. Street criminals typically purchase guns from neighborhood entrepreneurs who realize handsome profits smuggling guns from shops in states with lax laws for street-corner sales in cities with strict ones. A national waiting period could severely inhibit that deadly black market.

Beyond honoring his friendship with Mr. Brady, Mr. Reagan, a member of the N.R.A., makes clear that no one need be bullied by the big gun lobby when it strays from common sense. That's an act of leadership for President Bush to follow.

Analysis: This short editorial in the *New York Times* was classified as favorable toward Reagan. It shows that he, too, sees the urgent need to push for gun control legislation to end the violence plaguing American society today.

March 29, 1991. The story in this issue of the *Washington Post* says that former president Ronald Reagan returned to Washington yesterday to receive an honorary degree from the George Washington University (GWU). According to staff writer Donnie Radcliffe, Reagan provoked his George Washington University audience to cheers when he confirmed that he supports the so-called Brady bill, which would place a seven-day waiting period on handgun sales. Reagan, the story says, unleashed a few memories with his recollections of that March day 10 years ago when what he called "a routine public appearance came perilously close to being a very dark chapter in history." He lightened the mood considerably, according to the story, with his yarn about coming back to GWU, in whose hospital he nearly died of a gunshot wound to the chest. Radcliffe writes:

He'd been a little worried, he explained at a convocation conferring on him an honorary doctor of public service degree when he was told GWU wanted him back. At first, he said, he thought it was for a 10-year checkup, until his doctors in Los Angeles told him there was no such thing. Then he wondered if it had something to do with his hospital bill for the 12 days he spent there in 1981 recovering from the attempt on his life. The idea of 10 years' worth of interest, he said, had him prepared to plead his case:

"I'd recently lost my job. Before that I was living in public housing for a while. Then I learned I was to be given an honorary degree and that only made matters worse. You see," he confided, "I've been burdened by a sense of guilt because the first degree I received from my alma mater in 1932 was honorary.... Maybe if I had gone to school without the distraction of football, I would have done well and made something of myself."

The story notes that the emergency section of the GWU hospital, which was renamed the Ronald Reagan Institute of Emergency Medicine, was surrounded by the 65-member medical and administrative team that kept him going throughout his ordeal in March 1981. Present at the ceremony was Nancy Reagan, Reagan administration officials, and dignitaries, the story points out.

Analysis: This long, inside-page news story was coded as favorable. The public service award degree adds to the string of honorary degrees bestowed on Reagan over the years. It also shows that the former president still has some elements of wit and humor left in him as he uses an emotional moment to crack jokes, especially about how he lived in public housing (the White House), lost his job (the presidency), and was unable to earn a college degree the old-fashioned way (earn it through serious academics), and how playing football had distracted him from attaining a more fulfilling career.

June 30, 1991. This inside-page news story headlined "Reagan Requests Search of '80 Files" in the *New York Times* discusses how former president Ronald Reagan wants his 1980 campaign files searched for documents that might shed light on allegations that campaign officials conspired to delay the release of American hostages from Iran until after the presidential election. It quotes a letter that Reagan wrote to Ralph Bledsoe, director of the Ronald Reagan Presidential Library in Simi Valley, California, asking him to conduct the search with the help of an unnamed senior archivist from the National Archives and to make public any pertinent documents. Reagan notes in his letter: "Although I firmly believe these charges are groundless, I feel we should do all we can to clear the air of this unsubstantiated allegation." The *New York Times* story indicates how the U.S. Congress was considering a formal investigation of this allegation, which says that campaign officials might have dealt with Iranians to delay the release of 52 hostages until after the election in exchange for the promise of weapons. The story says that Reagan asked Bledsoe to look for records showing that "anyone associated with my campaign had contacts with Iranians or other foreign representatives in which a delay in the release of the hostages was discussed." Reagan was also quoted to have asked specifically for a search for records relating to the schedule and overseas travel by his campaign manager, William J. Casey, whom he later appointed director of the Central Intelligence Agency (CIA). Giving a background to the allegations, the news story says that they surfaced periodically in the 1980s and recently in an op-ed article in the *New York Times* by Gary Sick, a former Carter administration official, and in a book by Abolhassan Bani Sadr, the former president of Iran. Both men, according to the news story, contended that the Reagan–Bush campaign feared that release of the hostages before Election Day would damage Reagan's chances of victory, noting that the hostages were released within minutes of Reagan's taking office on January 20, 1981. Bill Garber, a Reagan spokesman, was quoted in this news story as saying that he did not know when the search would be completed.

Analysis: This medium-sized *New York Times* story was identified and coded as favorable because it enabled Reagan to present his side of the story regarding allegations about his possible involvement in the delay in releasing American hostages being held in Iran before the 1980 presidential election.

August 2, 1991. This story, which appeared in the *Washington Post*, talks about the decision to drop three longtime associates of former president Ronald Reagan from the board of the Ronald Reagan Presidential Foundation, which operates his presidential library. This story, written by *Post* staff writer Lou Cannon, says that Reagan has explained that he, not his wife, Nancy, was responsible for asking three trustees—Edwin Meese III, William P. Clark, and Martin Anderson—to leave the board. According to Cannon's story, Reagan said that he had decided "some time ago" that the three should leave the board when their six-year terms expired. "It was definitely my feeling that there ought to be a change," Reagan reportedly suggested. In this story, Reagan strongly denied a report in Thursday's *Washington Post* attributed to unnamed associates of the former president that Nancy Reagan had engineered a "purge" of the board members, who together have more than 65 years of service to Reagan. The story quotes Reagan as saying, "This is part of the picking on Nancy that goes on." He added, "She hasn't done any of these things that they accuse her of doing." Cannon recalls that during the Reagan presidency, Nancy Reagan was often targeted by staff members who had fallen out of favor as the source of their troubles. In the most publicized of these controversies, Cannon notes, she was blamed by Donald T. Regan for his ouster as White House chief of staff. The story, says Reagan, who telephoned the *Post* to take responsibility for the decision, offered no reason for it beyond his feeling that it was desirable to have a one-term limitation. He reportedly said that Meese, Clark, and Anderson would be replaced but that he was "not prepared to say" when this would happen or who the new trustees would be.

Analysis: This medium-length news story was classified as unfavorable. Even though it was meant to serve as a damage-control story, it reopened the bad publicity that surrounded Nancy Reagan regarding allegations that she had allegedly meddled in official White House activities and influenced most of Reagan's decision-making efforts.

PRESS PORTRAYAL OF BUSH

January, 21, 1993. This story provides a blow-by-blow account of the last day of George Bush in the White House. Bill McAllister and Ann Devroy of the *Washington Post* write that minutes after he had received a standing ovation for "his half-century of service to America," Bush stepped yesterday into the world of former presidents. The report says that a military honor guard lined the way for Bush and former first lady Barbara Bush from the otherwise deserted East Front of the Capitol to the waiting helicopter that would take them to Andrews Air Force Base and away from the city where they had lived for the last dozen years. According to the report, a few close aides and the new president (Bill Clinton) and vice president (Al Gore) were on hand to say good bye. But the big crowds were gone, says the report, a reminder of the sudden, swift transition to private citizen that can make a former president seem lonely and adrift. The report says that Bush's final hours as president were, in the words of former press secretary Marlin Fitzwater, "pretty emotional. There were a lot of goodbyes." The ending that once seemed to be so painfully slow to Bush, the report says, came swiftly as he bade farewell to telephone operators, declared 10 Arizona counties flood disaster areas, and then left the White House. "He's fine, a new life, looking forward to a new life," Fitzwater later told reporters as the former president left Andrews for Houston. According to the report, the Bushes will live there in a rented house until their new home is built later this year. The report says that Bush was stoic and solemn as he left Washington. He had advised some friends not to show up at the airport for his departure, the report points out, but he seemed delighted that several hundred youthful White House aides appeared anyway. "This is beyond the call, by golly," Bush reportedly said, as he grasped a few hands before climbing aboard the presidential jet. Bush's helicopter circled the Capitol and then the White House before flying to Andrews. The report says that the former president said nothing to the crowd there, but he stopped by an area where the White House aides were waiting as his two dogs, Millie and Ranger, scampered up a carpeted stairway and into the jet.

Analysis: This story was coded as long and neutral because it provided a well-balanced assessment of the final day of Bush in office. Among other things, Bush, visibly moved by his circumstance, reportedly failed to wave good-bye to the diehard fans and admirers who had gathered at Andrews Air Force Base to bid him farewell.

January 23, 1993. This feature article, written by Richard Harwood in the *Washington Post*, looks at the personal diaries of George Bush regarding the Iran–Contra affair. Harwood writes that authorities made public excerpts from the diaries ranging from 32 to 45 pages depending on which paper one reads—and 174 pages of deposition given by Bush to Iran–Contra prosecutors in January 1988. Harwood writes:

They dealt directly with a question that has hovered, buzzard-like, over Bush for several years: Had he been telling the truth or lying since 1986 about his involvement or noninvolvement in this affair? They were not, as it turned out, as colorful as some of the Nixon tapes from the Watergate era. But they addressed an issue in which the public had a major interest. So did the special counsel in this case, Lawrence E. Walsh, who has been implying in recent weeks that Bush was vulnerable to a prosecution involving these very documents.

Harwood points out that the documents were "made public" on Friday, January 15, in the sense that the White House turned them over to newspapers, magazines, radio, and television correspondents and whoever else qualified on that day as a member of the press corps. Harwood notes that the networks did not set aside time for "special reports" as they often do when important events occur. For example, he notes,

Time and Newsweek did not tear up their magazines that weekend to publish special sections on what the New York Times described as "the extraordinary stream-of-consciousness-monologue" contained within the Bush diary. In fact, by the Times's own standards, it gave short shrift to the materials, reprinting only 36 inches of excerpts.

Harwood also looks at how other newspapers treated the news about the diaries' release. According to him, the *Washington Post* "stripped the story across the top of its front page with a headline and opening paragraph suggesting that Bush was up to his neck in the Iran–Contra plot." However, the *Baltimore Sun*, Harwood says, interpreted the materials as a vindication of Bush but printed less than a column of excerpts, which was a few inches more than what the *Wall Street Journal* published. On its part, the *New York Times*, according to Harwood, noted that the diary portrays Bush as a "blindly loyal" lackey to Ronald Reagan. In summing up his article, Harwood notes: "The Bush diaries and depositions were not released for the entertainment and titillation of a handful of people who, because of some accident of history, happen to possess press cards. The public, which, among other things, paid for them, also has an interest in what they contain."

Analysis: This medium-length feature article was classified as neutral. It not only criticized the media for not reprinting enough of the diaries but also provided a divided opinion about how the press sees Bush's involvement in the whole Iran–Contra affair.

April 9, 1993. The headline on this *Los Angeles Times* news story filed from Kuwait city says it all: "Kuwait Prepares to Receive Bush the Liberator." Written by Mark Fineman, the story begins by saying that the "emir of Kuwait sent one of his best Boeing 747 passenger jets out for alterations this week—a royal bedroom suite, a formal dining room, several posh guest rooms and decor fit for a king." According to the story, this was standard travel fare for the leader of one of the world's richest nations. But the jumbo jet that Sheik Jabbar al Ahmed al Sabah took out of service from the Kuwait Airlines fleet was not for the emir, the story says, but for the man whom he and his 650,000 fellow Kuwaitis credit with the liberation of their oil-rich emirate, a singular national hero here: former president George Bush. The emir, the story notes, has arranged royal round-trip transportation for private citizen Bush, his wife, and sons and a host of former Bush administration officials, including former secretary of state James A. Baker III and his wife and former White House press secretary Marlin Fitzwater. They all are scheduled to arrive Tuesday in Kuwait city for a three-day "personal" visit. In this land, where one Kuwaiti intellectual said, "We still believe God is No. 1 and President Bush is No. 2," the whole country is making intense preparations for a national veneration. The story notes that the former president, who forged and commanded the 32-nation military coalition that drove Iraq from Kuwait two years ago, will be awarded degrees and national titles. Bush, the story points out, will be honored by the emirate's new, freely elected National Assembly and lavished with gifts. In his first high-profile trip since leaving the Oval Office—and his first visit to Kuwait since he helped free it from Iraqi occupation in 1991—Bush can expect the ego boost of a postpresidential lifetime, the story observes. Public proposals in Kuwait this week, according to the story, included declaring a national holiday in Bush's honor; closing Kuwait city's main, eight-lane highway for a parade of the hundreds of thousands of Kuwaitis who wish to show their gratitude to the former U.S. president, and a public appeal for the emir to designate a building where people can leave gifts for Bush. The story talks about how the Kuwaiti media paid glowing tribute to Bush, with the *Arab Times* saying: "He stood tall at the helm of his great nation and stood up to the Tyrant of the 20th Century."

Analysis: This medium-length news story was classified as favorable because Bush is hailed in it as the hero and as a liberator by the emir and people of oil-rich Kuwait.

June 22, 1993. This story in this day's issue of the *New York Times* talks about how former president George Bush wrote to inform the Republican National Committee today that he had decided not to accept a $12,500 monthly stipend from the party. However, the story notes that Bush's immediate predecessor, Ronald Reagan, receives the same amount. According to the story, Bush wrote a letter to the committee a short time after the party chairman, Haley Barbour, defended the payments, which were disclosed last week in *Business Week* magazine, to both former presidents as reimbursement for Republican political activities. The story says that the payment comes to $150,000 per year, or $2,000 more than the public pension granted to former presidents. The story quotes Barbour as saying that the party began making the payments to Reagan when he left office in January 1989 and extended the policy to Bush this year. But there is little demand for Bush's assistance from party members; indeed, many have criticized the way he conducted his reelection campaign last year, the story notes. In contrast, the story concludes, the Republican chairman said that Reagan frequently signs party fund-raising mail and makes appearances at party events.

Analysis: This short news story, in the inside pages of the *New York Times*, was classified as neutral. Although Bush may be saving the Republican National Committee some money by refusing the monthly stipend, some of the party's leaders are not entirely sure whether he was fully committed to the GOP.

September 1, 1993. The headline on this news item, which appeared in the *Los Angeles Times*, reads: "New Data Gives Bush Economic Figures a Boost." The news story, jointly written by Robert A. Rosenblatt and Greg Miller, quotes the Commerce Department as saying that economic growth was far more robust during the final year of George Bush's presidency than previously reported. Also the official figures suggested that the 1990–1991 recession was much milder than generally believed. The story says that the changed numbers, which represent a more accurate survey of activity at the nation's retail stores and shopping malls and updated corporate tax returns, show that consumer spending was substantially more buoyant in the months preceding Bush's defeat in November 1992 than believed at the time. The story suggests that the revisions overturn conventional beliefs about the nation's economy under Bush and the man who defeated him, President Bill Clinton. "Instead of showing an economy improving rather steadily from 1990–1991 recession, the latest numbers indicate that the economy rebounded sharply to a much slower rate under Clinton," the story says. Several people interviewed for this story also expressed surprise at the new survey results. For example, Martin Regalia, chief economist at the U.S. Chamber of Commerce, is reported as saying that the economy in 1992 "was doing significantly better than the Democrats were saying, but then the Democrats quit saying that the minute Clinton got elected." Also, Michael Penzer, senior economist at the Bank of America in San Francisco, is quoted as saying: "There must be people in the White House this morning [saying], 'Thank God these numbers weren't released during election.'" This *Los Angeles Times* story notes that Bush's enormous popularity after the military victory in the Persian Gulf War melted away in the face of the discouraging economic statistics. The story points out that although Clinton won, pounding hard the economic issue throughout the campaign, the Commerce Department's new numbers suggest that Bush's view of the economy was more accurate than many people realized.

Analysis: This long news story was classified as favorable to Bush. It exonerated him from the gloomier economic picture painted shortly before the 1992 presidential election in which he lost to Clinton.

December 1, 1993. This news story, appearing in the *New York Times*, states that Queen Elizabeth II of Great Britain has made former president George Bush a knight. The story says Bush received the Knight Grand Cross of the Order of the Bath yesterday from the queen in a ceremony in London. According to the story, it is the highest honor that Britain gives foreigners. Bush and his wife, Barbara, who were in London on a private visit, also had lunch with the queen and Prince Philip at Buckingham Palace. The story says that because he is not a British subject, Bush is not entitled to be known as Sir George, but he can use the initials G.C.B. after his name, noting that the initials almost match his monogram.

Analysis: This very short, inside-page news item was classified as favorable to Bush because the knighthood adds to his string of awards and honors and relates to the cordial relations that he enjoys with the British monarchy.

January 5, 1994. This *New York Times* article examines former president George Bush's newfound private life in Texas. It recounts how the Bushes insisted that they are utterly content to be in their new, red-brick house on West Oak Drive South in Houston, Texas. Writer Sam Howe Verhovek notes that "by returning here and building the two-and-half-story home on a modest lot in the affluent but hardly showy Tanglewood section, both Bushes take an obvious pleasure in demonstrating that they have done exactly what they always insisted they would do when the time came to leave Washington." The article says that although many doubted whether the Bushes were trading their New England home for Texas, their home was now indisputably in Texas, adding that the Bushes "have made a determined, if low-key, effort to blend in with the city where Mr. Bush sent some of his children to Poe Elementary School and which he represented as a two-term Congressman in the 1960's." The article refers to a letter that the Bushes faxed to a reporter saying, "We are living in our new house, built on our famous tiny lot, and it is perfect for us." The article mentions how the former president has frequently been seen dining at restaurants, cheering at Oilers and Rockets games, shopping for electronics in the Best Buy store, and posing briefly for pictures.

Analysis: This medium-length feature article was classified as favorable to Bush. It shows how the former president and his family have adjusted to their new private life and home in Houston, Texas.

September 13, 1994. The story in this day's issue of the *Los Angeles Times*, written by Bill Stall, reports how former president George Bush came to Santa Monica on Monday to raise $700,000 for Republican governor Pete Wilson's campaign. The story says that this occasion marked Bush's first political appearance in California since the 1992 election, in which he became the first Republican presidential candidate to fail to carry the state since Barry Goldwater in 1964. In his eight-minute luncheon address Bush reportedly praised U.S. Senate candidate Mike Huffington, a longtime Texas friend. According to the story, Huffington, who has been criticized as a virtual carpetbagger from Texas by his critics—including some Republicans—was described by the former president as "a good friend, a man who's fighting a superb battle for the Senate." Bush, an adopted Texan, reportedly said, "I am delighted that Mike Huffington is here, a man I've known for a long, long time," and "I strongly urge you to support Mike Huffington. He's a good man and he'll do well in the Senate." Standing at the podium at the Museum of Flying at the Santa Monica Airport, Bush is reported as saying that it is impressive "to feel this surge for the Wilson campaign. It's just wonderful." The story says that he praised Wilson for "an incredible record" on issues such as illegal immigration, welfare, crime control, and education, adding, while standing in front of a massive American flag, "In Pete, you have a fighter."

Analysis: This news story was identified as medium-length. It was classified as favorable because it depicted Bush's fund-raising skills and his ability to rally Republicans to support party activities.

February 28, 1995. The headline on this inside-page news item reads: "Bush Denied Control of His Record," and the subheadline goes: "Judge Voids Deal Signed With Archivist." Toni Locy, the *Washington Post* staff writer, says U.S. district judge Charles R. Richey yesterday declared "null and void" a controversial agreement signed in the waning hours of the Bush administration that gave the former president broad legal control of computerized records of his presidency. According to the story, the judge ruled that the agreement between Bush and then archivist Don W. Wilson on January 19, 1993, circumvented the Presidential Records Act, which abolished presidential ownership of White House records and was passed after Watergate and the fight over former president Richard M. Nixon's documents and tapes. Locy writes:

"Indeed, to hold otherwise would be to find that an agreement between the president and certain officials of the executive branch, signed on the last day of an administration, may supersede an act of Congress; such a notion, of course, is insupportable," Richey wrote in a 51-page opinion. "No one—not even a president—is above the law," he added.

According to the story, Richey called the agreement made by Wilson—who added to the controversy by becoming director of the George Bush Center at Texas A&M University—"arbitrary, capricious, an abuse of discretion, and contrary to Law." The story says that the judge ordered acting archivist, Trudy H. Peterson, not to honor the agreement, which the Clinton administration defended in court. Instead, the story says, the judge ordered Peterson to comply with the Presidential Records Act, which regulates presidential records during and after a president's term of office. The story explains that under this act, most presidential records become available to the public no later than five years after the archivist gets custody of them, noting: "Before leaving office, however, a president can impose restrictions on some sensitive documents for up to 12 years. The story points out that Bush did not sign the agreement as president but simply as "George Bush." The document also was not on White House stationery, nor was it time stamped, the judge reportedly said.

Analysis: This medium-length news story was classified as unfavorable because the judge ruled against Bush in this presidential records suit.

May 15, 1995. This commentary, written by Mickey Edwards, a former Republican congressman from Oklahoma, praises George Bush in the *Los Angeles Times* for resigning his lifetime membership in the gun lobbying group the National Rifle Association (NRA). He writes: "Hurray for George Bush. He may or may not have been a good president—history will almost certainly treat him better than the voters did—but he has been consistent on the important things: courage, compassion, character." Edwards describes as "stupid and mean-spirited" an NRA fund-raising letter that "equates federal agents with Nazi storm troopers...." He argues that although most members of the NRA are honest, law-abiding citizens," one can defend the rights of these men and women to use their weapons lawfully without following the NRA into the murky world of paranoia and craziness." He refers to NRA's many years of responsibly working for a cause that many Americans believed in, but notes: "Now it has gone over the edge, and it's time to join George Bush in drawing the line."

Analysis: This is a medium-length commentary that was classified as favorable for Bush. It casts him as both sensitive and pragmatic, willing to take action when forced to do so.

July 18, 1995. This news story, which appeared on page A19 in the *Washington Post*, reports about the official unveiling of former president George Bush's portrait in the White House. Ann Devroy, who covered the occasion, says that these portrait ceremonies are a recent addition to White House tradition, begun by Jimmy Carter when he invited the Republican whom he defeated, Gerald R. Ford, to the White House to see his portrait unveiled. The story says that Ronald Reagan did not do the same for Carter, whose portrait was hung without ceremony in 1983. But Bush, the story notes, picked up the gesture after inheriting the White House from Reagan, and Clinton continued. The story says that the Bushes' portraits, painted by Herbert Abrams, will remain in the East Room for a month, on view by tours. The president's portrait will be formally hung in the Grand Foyer on the state floor of the White House, and the first lady's in the main hallway near the Vermeil Room. The story notes that in a gracious salute, Clinton underscored some of the themes of Bush's four years in office—volunteerism, public service, and education—on which the two share common, although not identical ground. The story says that Clinton told the gathering that Bush's portrait [w]ill stand as a reminder of George Bush's basic integrity and decency and of his entire adult lifetime devoted to public service." Clinton is said to have saluted Bush not only for his leadership of the Persian Gulf War, the military triumph for which the president will perhaps be best remembered, but also for some of Bush's domestic agenda that Clinton, as a candidate, rarely acknowledged—including Bush's Points of Light program and supporting the Americans with Disabilities Act and the Clean Air Act, the two major pieces of domestic legislation bearing Bush's signature.

Analysis: Classified as medium in length, this news story was identified as favorable because it portrays the accomplishments of Bush and displays his official portrait among those of other U.S. presidents hanging in the White House.

September 12, 1995. This three-column headline in the World News section of the *Washington Post* reads: "Bush Urges Low-Key China Policy." In this report, filed from Beijing, Steven Mufson writes that former president George Bush today condemned American isolationists and urged "more consultation and... less confrontation" in U.S. policy toward China. The report says that Bush also expressed sympathy with China's troubles in hosting the international women's conference here this month. "I feel somewhat sorry for the Chinese having Bella Abzug running around China," Bush said of the former New York congresswoman, a leading figure at the 4th United Nations (UN) World Conference on Women, which ends Friday. "Bella Abzug is one who has always represented the extremes of the women's movement," Bush reportedly said. Bush's comments, according to the report, came on the heels of a tumultuous two weeks in which China has been accused of using heavy-handed security and surveillance to harass women attending the UN conference and a parallel forum of nongovernmental organizations that ended last week. The report says that Abzug accused Bush tonight of "taking cheap shots" at her and fired back, saying, "Poor George," recycling former Texas governor Ann Richards' words to the 1988 Democratic convention, "Seems he's still got the silver foot in his mouth." The report says that Bush's remarks came in a wide-ranging speech at a World Food Production Conference in Beijing as he continues an Asia tour that has taken him to Vietnam and will include a visit to Japan. According to the report, Bush, who was ambassador to China in 1974–75, said that many critics of China's rights record have lost perspective of the advances made over a longer period. He reportedly noted that China has "far more individual liberties" than when he was ambassador 20 years ago and also an "entrepreneurial spirit" that could help change political affairs. The report says that after the 1989 Chinese crackdown on massive democracy demonstrations in Beijing's Tiananmen Square, Bush as president battled to maintain trade diplomatic relations with China when many others sought more punitive measures. "I feel strongly about human rights, as all Americans do," Bush reportedly said, "but to think that cutting off trade privileges will make these countries do what we want made no sense to me whatsoever."

Analysis: This news story, classified as long, was also identified as neutral because it provided a balanced coverage of the war of words and ridicule between Bush and Abzug.

REFERENCES

Bergholz, R. (1977, December 3). Ford assails War Powers Act of 1974. *Los Angeles Times*, p. III 10.

Bird, D. (1977, March 24). Ford, in city, warns of Soviet buildup. *New York Times*, p. 3.

Bumiller, E. (1989, October 26). Sony may restore 'decency' to Hollywood, says Reagan. *Washington Post*, p. A1.

Bush rejects payments from Republican Party. (1993, June 22). *New York Times*, p. A14.

Cannon, L. (1991, February 7). The 8 decades of Ronald Reagan. *Washington Post*, pp. B1, B2.

Cannon, L. (1991, August 2). Reagan says Nancy didn't "purge" pals. *Washington Post*, pp. B1, B4.

Carter to get award. (1981, March 7). *New York Times*, p. 38.

Carter visits Gaza; New W. Bank protests erupt. *Los Angeles Times*, p. 14.

Chronicle. (1993, December 1). *New York Times*, p. B5.

Crewdson, J. M. (1978, June 5). Fast-paced Ford carries the word to Texas. *New York Times,* p. 16.

Dahlburg, J.-T. (1990, September 18). Reagan greeted with hearty bearhug by Gorbachev. *Los Angeles Times*, p. A4.

Devroy, A. (1995, July 18). Picture perfect day for Bushes at White House. *Washington Post*, p. A19.

Dodson, M. (1978, April 21). Ford attends seminars on drug, alcohol dependence. *Los Angeles Times*, p. I 3.

Edwards, M. (1995, May 15). Bush's call to arms for NRA members. *Los Angeles Times,* p. B5.

Exit Jimmy Carter. (1981, January 27). Letter to the editor in the *Washington Post*, p. A16.

Feinberg, L. (1978, December 14). Ford has wide-ranging exchange with students. *Washington Post*, p. A2.

Fineman, M. (1993, April 9). Kuwait prepares to receive Bush the liberator. *Los Angeles Times*, p. A5.

For the Record. (1983, August 7). *Washington Post*, p. C6.

Ford asks Michigan to help his museum. (1977, May 26). *New York Times*, p. II 5.

Ford will appear on NBC programs about presidency. (1977, January 30). *New York Times*, p. I 3.

Frammolino, R. (1990, February 1). Ban on false endorsements pushed. *Los Angeles Times*, pp. A3, A25.

Harwood, R. (1993, January 23). A quick peek at the Bush diaries. *Washington Post*, p. A19.

Jimmy Carter lands to warm welcome from grateful China. (1981, August 25). *Washington Post*, p. A20.

Kempster, N. (1990, February 10). Reagan agrees to videotaped testimony in Poindexter trial. *Los Angeles Times*, p. A2.

Lardner, G., Jr. (1981, January 24). Records of the Carter presidency trucked on down to Georgia. *Washington Post*, p. A3.

Locy, T. (1995, February 28). Bush denied control of his records; judge voids deal signed with archivist. *Washington Post*, p. A17.

McAllister, B., & Devroy, A. (1993, January 21). For Bush, a day of solemn ritual and emotional goodbyes. *Washington Post*, pp. A1, A27.

McDowell, E. (1989, January 26). Reagan agrees to write memoirs. *New York Times*, p. C21.

McManus, D. (1982, October 11). Carter says U.S. agents infiltrated Iran. *Los Angeles Times,* p. I 15.

McQueen, M., & Weil, M. (1982, May 2). Carter blames Reagan for "hardship"; calls for Democratic unity. *Washington Post*, pp. B1, B7.

Mohr, C. (1982, January 7). On fly fishing: By Jimmy Carter. *New York Times*, p. 20.

Morrison, P. (1990, April 13). Off the wall; chunk of the Berlin barrier unveiled at Reagan Library. *Los Angeles Times*, pp. A3, A37.

Mr. Reagan finally leads on guns. (1991, March 29). *New York Times* editorial, p. A22.

Mufson, S. (1995, September 12). Bush urges low-key China policy. *Washington Post*, p. A12.

Nemy, E. (1983, July 14). A small Blue Ridge pine cabin is the Carters' rustic retreat. *New York Times*, pp. C1, C6.

Parks, M. (1981, August 26). Carter reminds Reagan of one-China commitment. *Los Angeles Times*, p. I 6.

Radcliffe, D. (1991, March 29). The first patient's return; a decade after assassination attempt, Reagan at GWU. *Washington Post*, pp. B1, B3.

Reagan requests search of '80 files; says he wants to "clear the air" on hostages in Iran. (1991, June 30). *New York Times*, p. 12.

Reeves, R. (1990, November 4). His turn. *Los Angeles Times Book Review*, pp. 1, 8.

Reston, J. (1978, February 19). A talk with Jerry Ford. *New York Times*, p. E17.

Rosenblatt, R. A., & Miller, G. (1993, September 1). New data gives Bush economic figures a boost. *Los Angeles Times*, pp. A1, A22.

Russell, M. (1979, October 20). Ford eliminates self as "active" candidate in '80. *Washington Post*, pp. A1, A6.

Shifrin, C. (1977, December 20). Ford stresses need for regulatory reform. Washington *Post*, pp. D1, D10.

Shogan, R. (1978, December 14). Ford warns of erosion in presidential authority. *Los Angeles Times*, pp. 12, 13.

Stall, B. (1994, September 13). Bush raises $700,000 for Wilson, gives Huffington praise. *Los Angeles Times*, pp. A3, A5.

"Unmuzzled" Ford rips Carter plans. (1977, May 20). *Los Angeles Times*, p. I 20.

Verhovek, S. H. (1994, January 5). No more Mr. President, just a Texas nice guy. *New York Times*, p. A10.

Virgin Isles vacation for Carters. *New York Times*, p. A17.

Chapter 5

Summary and Conclusion

REVIEW OF THE STUDY: THE COMPLETE PICTURE

This study critically and systematically examined how each of four ex-presidents, Gerald Ford, Jimmy Carter, Ronald Reagan, and George Bush, was treated in the press for three years after leaving the White House. This study provides clear evidence demonstrating that the ex-presidents continue to receive press coverage despite being out of office, but the degree of coverage is dependent on how busy that particular ex-president is and how much media contact he initiates as a result.

The study used both quantitative and qualitative content analysis techniques to investigate the content and tone of ex-presidential news from three leading, influential American newspapers—the *Los Angeles Times*, the *New York Times*, and the *Washington Post*. Content analysis could help measure the importance that the newspapers attach to ex-presidential news stories by noting the intensity and frequency with which they carry such stories. The study periods were Ford, 1977–1979; Carter, 1981–1983; Reagan, 1989–1991; Bush, 1993–1995. The basic unit of analysis was a story about the ex-presidents, and effort was made to determine the frequency of press coverage, the type of story, the major subject category of the story, the length and placement of the story, and the general tone of the story. In all, a sample of 380 stories was analyzed. This figure represents approximately one-fourth of all the stories that the three newspapers published about the ex-presidents during the first three years after they left office.

The patterns in ex-presidential news coverage suggest that while the number of stories increased during the first year of a president's leaving office, the number then progressively declined. The study results also show that the ex-president with the highest level of postpresidential activity received the largest number of stories in the press. Ford in his early retirement years was the most active; hence, he received the highest coverage of 31.6 percent (120 stories), with Reagan not very far behind with 30.0 percent (114 stories). Carter received the third highest story percentage of 27.9 (106 stories), and Bush received the least percentage of only 10.5 (40 stories). Although the study shows that Ford was busy in the first three years after he left office, Carter arguably is now the busiest of all four ex-presidents because of his vigorous humanitarian and international peace efforts concerning suffering and troubled parts of the world.

The study found that the newspapers emphasized straight news stories over the other five story-type categories: editorial, feature/commentary, letter to the editor, book review, and cartoon. Also, the study found that an overwhelming majority of ex-presidential stories appeared in the inside pages, and they were mostly medium-length in space size. Reagan received the largest number of inside-page stories (106), followed by Ford (104), Carter (93), then Bush (37).

Without a doubt coverage of all four ex-presidents was largely favorable in tone. Ford received the largest number of favorable stories, followed by Carter, Reagan, and Bush in that order. Where the story was not favorable, the tone was more often neutral, rather than negative. The three newspapers did a good job balancing the stories, often providing context, background, or a differing view. For example, stories about the Iran–Contra trial which focused mostly on Reagan, provided arguments from both the prosecution and defence lawyers. Also, the study looked at the tone of ex-presidential stories to determine the degree to which each subject subcategory was treated as favorable, neutral, or unfavorable. The results suggest that political issues received more favorable rating in the newspapers, than, say, judiciary or health matters.

The study also qualitatively analyzed 48 stories, 12 for each president, to assess their tone and nature. Brief analyses were then provided at the end of each story. This method was important because it complemented the quantitative analysis in determining and explaining the level of coverage given ex-presidential stories in the three American newspapers studied. Generally, the story coverage ranged from vacation and foreign trips, to award presentations, opening of a presidential museum-library, and political party fund-raising events. Like the quantitative results, most of the stories had a favorable tone.

Furthermore, the study provides brief biographical insights, and Chapter 6 gives a descriptive review of selected books published by and about the ex-presidents. A total of 446 annotated entries is provided here to help researchers and students. The brief biographies and the selected books provide interesting insights into the life and times of these four U.S. ex-presidents.

CONCLUDING THOUGHTS

As noted earlier, this study analyzed ex-presidential stories to learn what kinds of press treatment they are getting now that they are out of public office and are private citizens. The amount of press coverage that an ex-president receives largely depends on the type of postpresidential schedule that he draws up after leaving office. An ex-president has to be active to become an important "continuing story," not the other way round when he was the one mostly calling the shots from the White House. At this early transitional stage, the press also is keenly interested in knowing what the ex-president is doing in retirement and how he is adjusting to his new life. Once this curiosity is satisfied, the number of news stories progressively declines over time. But generally, the amount of press coverage that an ex-president receives depends to a large extent on how he wants to spend the rest of his life: either take it easy and avoid media spotlight or continue working toward the goals in which he believes in the hopes of drawing both media and public attention to them. Certainly, an ex-president with a rigorous agenda is bound to capture more media attention than one with a less rigorous postpresidential schedule.

As this study aptly suggests, the initiative of the ex-president himself was necessary to get his views and activities into the press. If he does not want to be bothered, the press stands little chance of intruding into his privacy. Thus, the relationship between the press and the ex-presidents is much more cordial and less adversarial than previously, when the men were chief executives with tremendous policy and decision-making powers. This time around the ex-president determines the extent of press coverage that he desires, not the press. What this means is that once out of office, the ex-presidents do have considerable control over the way that the press covers them.

Chapter 6

Major Books by and about the Ex-Presidents

This chapter presents 446 annotated books by and about former presidents Gerald Ford, Jimmy Carter, Ronald Reagan, and George Bush. The books include those written by the ex-presidents themselves as well as those by their former administration officials, family members, journalists, scholars, researchers, and experts.

GERALD FORD

1. Aaron, J. (1975). *Gerald R. Ford: President of destiny.* New York: Fleet Press.

    Filled with picture illustrations, this book provides a glimpse of the life and times of President Gerald Ford.

2. American Enterprise Institute. (1987). *A discussion with Gerald R. Ford: The American presidency.* Washington, D.C.: Author.

    In this volume, Ford offers his perspective on the American presidency, telling how it appeared during his long career in Congress and how it appears in retrospect.

3. Cannon, J. M. (1993). *Time and chance: Gerald Ford's appointment with history.* New York: HarperCollins.

    This book focuses on Ford's critical years from 1968 to 1976, providing a portrait of his early life and presidency. Among the major issues that the author tackles are Ford's ascendancy to the presidential office after Nixon's resignation, the Watergate scandal, and the facts surrounding Ford's controversial decision to grant a pardon to Nixon.

4.   Casserly, J. J. (1977). *The Ford White House: The diary of a speechwriter.* Boulder, CO: Colorado Associated University Press.

In this book, the author records not only events that occurred in the Ford White House but why they occurred. It argues that though Ford proves to be an imperfect president, God has not created the perfect politician.

5.   Collins, D. R. (1990). *Gerald R. Ford, 38th president of the United States.* Ada, OK: Garrett Educational Corp.

This book provides an insightful look at both the private and public lives of President Ford.

6.   Congressional Quarterly (CQ). (1974). *President Ford: The man and his record.* Washington, D.C.: Author.

Presents Ford's political activities, policies, and speeches and narrates events leading to his ascension to power.

7.   Coyen, J. R. (1979). *Fall in and cheer.* New York: Doubleday.

The former speechwriter of President Gerald Ford writes about his life and his experiences in the Ford White House.

8.   Doyle, M. V. (Ed.). (1973). *Gerald R. Ford: Selected speeches.* Arlington, VA: R. W. Beatty.

This volume, which also includes a brief biography, contains selected representative speeches made by Ford, during the period from 1965 through 1972.

9.   Facts on File. (1979). *Political profiles: The Nixon–Ford years.* New York: Author.

Provides biographies of Nixon and Ford including detailed accounts of their careers between 1969 and 1976.

10.   Firestone, B. J., & Ugrinsky, A. (Eds.). (1992). *Gerald R. Ford and the politics of post Watergate America.* Westport, CT: Greenwood Press.

This two-volume collection of essays, presented at the Hofstra University Presidential Conference on Gerald R. Ford, focuses on such issues as the pardon of Richard Nixon, the Rockefeller vice presidency, Middle East diplomacy, economic policy, and Ford's relations with the press.

11.   Firestone, B. J., & Ugrinsky, A. (Eds.). (1993). *Gerald R. Ford and the politics of post Watergate America.* Westport, CT: Greenwood Press.

This two-volume book, the result of a Hofstra University conference on the presidency of Gerald R. Ford, provides a comprehensive portrait of him as an individual and treats his administration.

12.   Ford, B. (With Chris Chase). (1979). *Betty Ford: The times of my life.* New York: Harper & Row.

Former U.S. first lady Betty Ford tells the story of the times of her life, her family, and how they wound up in the White House.

13.   Ford, G. R. (1978). *Toward a healthy economy.* Washington, D.C.: American Enterprise Institute.

This booklet contains a speech that Ford delivered on December 20, 1977, at the Francis Boyer lecture in Washington, D.C., dealing with his visions of restoring a strong, steadily growing economy.

14.   Ford, G. R. (1979). *A time to heal: The autobiography of Gerald R. Ford.* New York: Harper & Row.

In this book President Ford provides a candid view of his life and his years as the 38th president of the United States.

15.   Ford, G. R. (1987). *Humor and the presidency.* New York: Arbor House.

This book originated out of a two-day conference that brought together several personalities, including politicians, entertainers, and cartoonists, to the Ford Presidential Library and Museum in Grand Rapids, Michigan, to discuss humor and the presidency.

16.   Ford, G. R. (1998). *Greater Grand Rapids: City that works.* Memphis, TN: Towery.

In this book, filled with many photographs, former President Ford provides a complete and vivid description of Grand Rapids, Michigan, where he grew up. Shows how the town shaped his distinguished career later in life.

17.   Ford, G. R., & Stiles, J. R. (1965). *Portrait of the assassin*. New York: Simon & Schuster.

This book is a narrative account of the work of the Warren Commission, which investigated the assassination of President John F. Kennedy in 1963.

18.   Greene, J. R. (1992). *The limits of power: The Nixon and Ford administrations*. Bloomington: Indiana University Press.

This book examines political events of the years 1969 to 1977, covering the Nixon and Ford presidencies—the period when many Americans sought limits on the powers of the president and proceeded to put such limits into effect.

19.   Greene, J. R. (1994). *Gerald R. Ford: A bibliography*. Westport, CT: Greenwood Press.

This volume is a comprehensive compilation of the material pertaining to the life and political career of Gerald R. Ford. It contains more than 350 references to manuscript material on the Ford years, as well as monographs, journal articles, and memoir sources, including the first full listing of Ford's own writings available in print, oral histories, historiographical materials, and audiovisual materials.

20.   Greene, J. R. (1995). *The presidency of Gerald R. Ford*. Lawrence: University Press of Kansas.

This book analyzes President Ford's success in healing America as a nation and in establishing his administration during his tenure as the 38th U.S. president from 1974 to 1976. Conclusions in this book are based on Ford's personal and governmental papers and over 100 interviews with members of the Ford administration.

21.   Hartmann, R. T. (1980). *Palace politics: An insider's account of the Ford years*. New York: McGraw-Hill.

This book explores the activities of the White House staff, "the Pretorians," who wanted President Ford to change his persona. It argues that though Ford was a "good" president, his presidency was too short to know whether he would have been a "great" president.

22.   Head, R. G., Short, F. W., & McFarlane, R. C. (1978). *Crisis resolution: Presidential decision making in the Mayaguez and Korean confrontations*. Boulder, CO: Westview Press.

Using the S.S. *Mayaguez* seizure and the Korean demilitarized zone kill-ings of Americans as case studies, this book examines the Ford administration's crisis behavior and crisis management styles in presi-dential politics.

23. Hersey, J. (1975). *The president: A minute-by-minute account of a week in the life of Gerald Ford*. New York: Alfred A. Knopf.

The author uses his uninhibited access to the White House to gather ma-terial and information about President Gerald R. Ford through a work week in March 1975.

24. Howell, D., Howell, M-M., & Kronman, R. (1980). *Gentlemanly atti-tudes: Jerry Ford and the campaign of 1976*. Washington, D.C.: HKJV Publications.

This book gives an account of the inner workings of the 1976 campaign machine of incumbent Jerry Ford and takes a close look at him person-ally.

25. Hyland, W. (1987). *Mortal rivals: Superpower relations from Nixon to Reagan*. New York: Random House.

The former official in the U.S. State Department and on the National Security Council under the Ford administration provides information about his activities, focusing on Soviet–American relations, détente, and ballis-tic missile talks.

26. Kissinger, H. (1999). *Years of renewal*. New York: Simon & Schuster.

This is a final volume of Kissinger's memoirs covering his service as secretary of state in the Ford administration.

27. Kraus, S. (Ed.). (1979). *The great debates: Carter vs. Ford*. Bloomington: Indiana University Press.

This volume, among other things, examines the events and actions that brought about the 1976 Carter–Ford debates, investigates the way that the electorate perceived the debates, and assesses the effect that they had on voting decisions and on the presidential campaign generally.

28. Laackman, B. H. (1982). *Gerald R. Ford's scouting years*. Grand Rapids, MI: Kindel Ford Chapter, National Eagle Scout Association.

This book provides an insight into Ford's affiliations with the Boy Scouts of America as far back as 1924.

29.   LeRoy, D. (1974). *Gerald Ford—Untold story*. Arlington, VA: R. W. Beatty.

       Provides the background, the legislative record, and the thinking of Vice President Gerald Ford.

30.   Lurie, R. R. (1975). *Pardon me, Mr. President*. New York: Quadrangle/ New York Times Book.

       This book contains political cartoons depicting the Ford years.

31.   MacDougall, M. (1977). *We almost made it*. New York: Crown.

       An advertisement agent writes about his experiences in helping to run Ford's advertising campaign during his 1976 presidential bid.

32.   Mackaman, F. H. (1994). *Gerald R. Ford: Presidential perspectives from the National Archives*. Washington, D.C.: National Archives & Records Administration.

       Presents the life and political career of Ford, the 38th president of the United States.

33.   Mollenhoff, C. R. (1976). *The man who pardoned Nixon*. New York: St. Martin's Press.

       The author takes a critical look at Gerald Ford's background and his first 19 months in the White House and examines his record on many crucial issues.

34.   Nessen, R. (1978). *It sure looks different from the inside*. Chicago: Playboy Press.

       The former press secretary to President Gerald Ford writes about his experience and observations of the Ford administration.

35.   Osborne, J. (1977). *White House watch: The Ford years*. Washington, D.C.: New Republic Books.

       Provides insight into the first 19 months of Ford's administration.

36.   Randolph, S. G. (1987). *Gerald R. Ford, president*. New York: Walker.

        Filled with interesting pictures, this little book looks at the early life and
        public career of Jerry Ford.

37.   Reeves, R. (1975). *A Ford, not a Lincoln*. New York: Harcourt Brace
        Jovanovich.

        This book primarily looks at the first 100 days of Jerry Ford as president
        of the United States. The author also uses the book to tell us what he has
        learned about American politics and leadership in his 10 years as a news-
        paper reporter and magazine writer.

38.   Reichley, A. (1981). *Conservatives in an age of change: The Nixon and
        Ford administrations*. Washington, D.C.: Brookings Institution Press.

        The author argues that there are distinguishable traditions of conserva-
        tive ideology in American political history and examines its effects on
        policy in the administrations of Richard Nixon and Gerald Ford.

39.   Riegle, D. (1972). *O Congress*. New York: Doubleday.

        The author, a Republican from Michigan, provides a diary about the party's
        activities between April 1971 and March 1972 and includes material about
        Ford's leadership of the House Republicans.

40.   Rozell, M. J. (1992). *The press and the Ford presidency*. Ann Arbor: Uni-
        versity of Michigan Press.

        This book attempts to identify and assess the national journalistic evalu-
        ations of the Ford presidency, arguing that journalists play a central role
        in the development of a presidential image.

41.   Schapsmeier, E. L., & Schapsmeier, F. H. (Eds.). (1989). *Gerald Ford's
        date with destiny: A political biography*. New York: Peter Lang.

        This biography presents a narrative of Ford's life and political career. It
        argues that although Ford entered the White House in the aftermath of
        two national traumas, the Vietnam War and the Watergate scandal, he
        managed, despite his brief tenure, to heal the nation's divisive wounds
        and to conduct the affairs of the state with calm leadership.

42.   Sidey, H. (Photographs by Fred Ward). (1975). *Portrait of a president*.
        New York: Harper & Row.

This is a brief portrait of President Gerald R. Ford during his first months in the White House.

43.   Storing, H. J. (Ed.). (1986). *The Ford White House: A Miller Center conference chaired by Herbert J. Storing*. Lanham, MD: University Press of America.

In this volume, officials who actually worked with President Gerald R. Ford and those scholars who have studied the workings of the chief executive's office reflect on events at the White House after the upheaval brought on by the Watergate scandal.

44.   TerHorst, J. F. (1974). *Gerald Ford and the future of the presidency*. New York: Third Press.

The former press secretary in the Ford administration provides insights into his career and reasons for resigning his position after Ford pardoned Nixon over the Watergate scandal.

45.   Thompson, K. W. (1988). *The Ford presidency: Twenty-two intimate perspectives of Gerald R. Ford*. Lanham, MD: University Press of America.

Relying on oral historical study, this book helps in navigating the thickets of historical analysis and interpretation of President Ford's stewardship and evaluates whether or not it was an unfinished presidency.

46.   Vestal, B. (1974). *Jerry Ford, up close: An investigative biography*. New York: Coward, McCann, & Geohegan.

Written before his ascendancy to the presidency, this book looks at Jerry Ford the man, what kind of man he is, and what kind of president he would be.

47.   White House Office of Communications. (1976). *The Ford presidency: A portrait of the first two years*. Washington, D.C.: Author.

This volume primarily reports on the Ford administration's accomplishments.

48.   Winter-Berger, R. N. (1974). *The Gerald Ford letters*. Secaucus, NJ: L. Stuart.

The author, a lobbyist, attempts to set the record straight regarding his contacts with Ford during 1966 and 1968 and discusses alleged cash payments that he made to Ford.

JIMMY CARTER

49.   Abernathy, M. G., Hill, D. M., & Williams, P. (Eds.). (1984). *The Carter years: The president and policy making.* New York: St. Martin's Press.

        This book shows the contradictions and complexities of the modern presidency, particularly the constraints that Carter faced in pursuing his policy objectives.

50.   Adams, B., & Kavanagh-Baran, K. (1979). *Promise and performance: Carter builds a new administration.* Lexington, MA: Lexington Books.

        This study examines the process by which President Jimmy Carter made his key appointments during the first year of his administration.

51.   Adler, B. (Ed.). (1977). *The wit and wisdom of Jimmy Carter.* Secaucus, NJ: Citadel Press.

        Selected speeches, writings, press conferences, interviews, and conversations of the 39th president of the United States. Here Jimmy Carter talks freely, often with wit, candor, and honesty, about his faith, his family, his hopes, his fears, and his dreams.

52.   Allen, G. (1976). *Jimmy Carter, Jimmy Carter.* Seal Beach, CA: '76 Press.

        This book looks behind the myths that surround the peanut farmer from Plains, Georgia, Jimmy Carter, who became an American president.

53.   Anderson, P. (1994). *Electing Jimmy Carter: The campaign of 1976.* Baton Rouge: Louisiana State University Press.

        The author, Carter's chief speechwriter, draws on his memories and personal notes to write a memoir about the president's 1976 presidential campaign. This book is an intensely personal, partisan, novelistic view of Jimmy Carter and his first race for the presidency.

54.   Ariail, D., & Heckler-Feltz, C. (1996). *The carpenter's apprentice: The spiritual biography of Jimmy Carter.* Grand Rapids, MI: Zondervan.

        This is a personal, spiritual biography of Carter told by his pastor and family.

55.   Baker, J. T. (1977). *A southern Baptist in the White House.* Philadelphia: Westminster Press.

This book argues why and how Carter's southern Baptist upbringing would prove a positive force in his presidency. It explores the religious context that powerfully influences Carter as well as provides a new understanding of the southern Baptist tradition.

56.   Benze, J. G., Jr. (1987). *Presidential power and management techniques: The Carter and Reagan administrations in historical perspective.* Westport, CT: Greenwood Press.

The study looks at the historical trend toward centralization of policy implementation in the president's office and shows how—and with what degree of success—the Reagan and Carter administrations have met this problem.The book includes empirical data provided on the presidency and the analysis of both change and continuity between administrations in the handling of specific management areas.

57.   Bitzer, L., & Rueter, T. (1980). *Carter vs. Ford: The counterfeit debates of 1976.* Madison: University of Wisconsin Press.

This book provides accurate and readable transcripts of the Ford–Carter debates of 1976. It addresses the questions: What was wrong with the Ford–Carter debates? How can future debates be improved?

58.   Boehme, R. (With Rus Walton). (1976). *What about Jimmy Carter?* Washington, D.C.: Third Century.

This tiny book basically explores the question: Who would most closely administer and legislate so that God's principles are made manifest in our federal government in the coming years? Specifically, it looks at Carter's religious background vis-à-vis his ability to provide spiritual leadership to America.

59.   Bourne, P. G. (1997). *Jimmy Carter: A comprehensive biography from Plains to post presidency.* New York: Scribner.

This book presents a portrait of Jimmy Carter, arguing that he became president during a time of remarkable change and turmoil, receiving little credit for managing those difficult times and for healing the nation after a period of profound trauma.

60.   Brinkley, D. (1999). *The unfinished presidency: Jimmy Carter's journey beyond the White House.* New York: Penguin.

This book documents Carter's activities around the world, calling him "a true citizen of the world." The book provides a detailed portrait of his tireless efforts to negotiate peace in trouble spots around the world and of his relationship to Presidents George Bush and Bill Clinton.

61.   Brzezinski, Z. (1983). *Power and principle: Memoir of the national security adviser, 1977–1981*. New York: Farrar, Straus, & Giroux.

The author explores in depth those central issues of American policy that were his main concern while serving as the national security adviser in the Carter administration.

62.   Callahan, D. M. (1979). *Jimmy, the story of young Jimmy Carter.* Garden City, NY: Doubleday.

A look at the young life and times of Jimmy Carter and his vision to become president of the United States.

63.   Campagna, A. S. (1995). *Economic policy in the Carter administration*. Westport, CT: Greenwood Press.

The book posits that Carter took office at an unfortunate time, when America's economy was floundering, but as he set to solving it, he abandoned the traditional Democratic agenda and became a forerunner of Reagan. In the end, the book argues, Carter did not conquer inflation but sacrificed instead his ambitious programs for restructuring government, crafting a lasting energy program, and reforming the tax structure, welfare, and health care.

64.   Campbell, C. S. J. (1988). *Managing the presidency: Carter, Reagan, and the search for executive harmony*. Pittsburgh: University of Pittsburgh Press.

This is a comparative study of the records of Presidents Carter and Reagan to illustrate how their policies and personal behaviors assisted in defining both the political agenda and the effectiveness of the presidency as an institution.

65.   Carter, J. (1975). *Addresses of Jimmy Carter, governor of Georgia: 1971–1975*. Atlanta: Georgia Department of Archives and History.

This is a collection of speeches and addresses Carter delivered during his tenure as governor of Georgia.

66.   Carter, J. (1977). *Why not the best?* Nashville, TN: Broadman Press.

This autobiographical book, based on Carter's personal observations and experiences, sums up his opinions about America and how relevant they are to values that most Americans want to see involved at the top levels of the country's national leadership.

67.   Carter, J. (1982). *Keeping faith: Memoirs of a president*. New York: Bantam Books.

This book provides an overriding impression of Carter during his term as the 39th president of the United States. According to Carter, the narrative is not a history of his administration but a highly personal report of his own experience filled with gratitude and pleasure and with a few painful memories.

68.   Carter, J. (1984). *Negotiation, the alternative to hostility*. Macon, GA: Mercer University Press.

This booklet contains the inaugural address of the Carl Vinson memorial lecture series delivered by Carter at Mercer University in Macon, Georgia.

69.   Carter, J. (1985). *The blood of Abraham: Insights into the Middle East*. Boston: Houghton Mifflin.

In this book Jimmy Carter makes an effort to relate current Middle East politics to the Bible and the Koran.

70.   Carter, J. (1988). *An outdoor journal: Adventures and reflections*. Fayetteville: University of Arkansas Press.

In this book former President Jimmy Carter recounts his childhood days in Plains, Georgia, where he bonded with the environment and how his activities outdoors nurtured his love and respect for the natural world.

71.   Carter, J. (1992). *Turning point: A candidate, a state, and a nation come of age*. New York: Times Books.

Ex-president Jimmy Carter tells the story of how he first sought public office in 1962 and how the social and political conflicts in the South during that era shaped his vision of how people of good faith can join forces to right the wrongs of American society.

72.   Carter, J. (1994). *Always a reckoning, and other poems*. New York: Times Books.

This is a collection of poetry by former President Jimmy Carter, who shares his private memories about his childhood, his family, and political life with the reader.

73.   Carter, J. (1995). *The little baby Snoogle-Fleejer.* New York: Times Books.

With illustrations by his daughter, Amy, former president Jimmy Carter writes his first children's book about how Young Jeremy, who cannot walk, is abandoned at the seashore one day when others flee at the sight of a terrifying sea monster. As Jeremy confronts this horror, he is surprised to find a kindred spirit in the little baby Snoogle-Fleejer.

74.   Carter, J. (1995). *Talking peace: A vision for the next generation.* New York: E. P. Dutton Children's Books.

This book, the first by a former U.S. president to address younger readers, provides personal narrative and thoughtful exposition of current history, particularly the causes and effects of conflict, and explains the urgent call for nonviolent conflict resolution in the world today.

75.   Carter, J. (1996). *A government as good as its people.* Fayetteville: University of Arkansas Press.

In this book Carter presents an unpretentious account of how he and his wife, Rosalynn, created a new full life after their challenging and rewarding years in the White House. Drawing upon their own experiences and those of many others, the Carters propose dozens of ways for any couple in career transition to renew their commitment to themselves and to life.

76.   Carter, J. (1997). *Sources of strength: Meditations on scripture for a living faith.* New York: Times Books.

In this book Carter presents his favorite 52 Bible meditations as a source of inspiration and strength in everyday life situations—good or bad.

77.   Carter, J. (1998). *Living faith.* New York: Times Books.

Drawing on his experience, the former U.S. president explores the values closest to his heart and the personal and spiritual beliefs that have nurtured and sustained him. This book is filled with compelling stories about people whose lives have touched his—some from the world stage, more from modest walks of life.

78.   Carter, J. (1998). *The virtues of aging.* New York: Ballantine Books.

In this book former president Jimmy Carter passionately explores the physical aspect of aging and the prejudice that exists toward the elderly. More important, Carter shares the knowledge and the pleasures that age have brought him.

79.   Carter, J. (2001). *An hour before daylight: Memories of a rural boyhood.* New York: Simon & Shuster.

In his latest book the former president writes about his childhood life on a Georgia farm and the circumstances that shaped his character, including the Depression, his parents, and his association with his many black neighbors.

80.   Carter, J. & Carter, R. (1987). *Everything to gain: Making the most of the rest of your life.* New York: Random House.

In this book, President Carter and his wife, Rosalynn, tell us some of the most traumatic experiences of their lives. They narrate how they used the experiences of their own family and friends to illustrate the challenges and achievements as well as the problems and failures that most people have to expect.

81.   Carter, R. (1984). *First lady from Plains.* Boston: Houghton Mifflin.

Offers insight into the life and times of the 39th first lady of the United States, from early years in the rural South, to her days in Georgia's political limelight, to her activities in the White House and in international affairs.

82.   Collins, T. (1976). *The search for Jimmy Carter.* Waco, TX: Word Books.

Filled with pictures, this book explores Jimmy Carter's life, his family background, his complexity as a person, and his potential for presidential greatness.

83.   Congressional Quarterly (CQ). (1980). *President Carter 1980.* Washington, D.C.: Author.

This book, one in many of CQ's presidency series, describes Carter's last year in office, focusing on economic, foreign, and national security problems. It also includes major Carter messages, news conference transcripts, major executive branch nominations, and Congressional Quarterly's annual presidential support study.

84.　　*The cumulated indexes to the public papers of the presidents of the United States, Jimmy Carter, 1977–1981.* (1983). Millwood, NY: Kraus International.

This volume offers a unique view of the Carter presidency by examining the character of the president and the individuals with whom he interacted, as well as the historical events that were shaped by the president and that, in turn, shaped his presidency.

85.　　Debyshire, I. (1987). *Politics in the United States: From Carter to Reagan.* Edinburgh, UK: W&R Chambers.

Examines the changing political scene in the United States during the Carter and Reagan eras and the different policy programs pursued by each of them.

86.　　DeMause, L., & Ebel, H. (1977). *Jimmy Carter and American fantasy: Psychohistorical explorations.* New York: Institute of Psychohistory Press.

This study focuses on Carter's childhood years, exploring what strengths and weaknesses he acquired during his formative years from his relationship with his parents and other caretakers and what personality traits and general patterns of behavior have remained dominant throughout his life. The study also focuses on historical group-fantasy which, among other things, tries to determine the mood of America and explores how people feel about their leaders and the actual condition of the country.

87.　　Dumbrell, J. (1993). *The Carter presidency: A re-evaluation.* Manchester, UK: Manchester University Press.

This book generally focuses on Jimmy Carter's principal 1976 campaign theme, "competence and compassion," by examining the president's human rights policy.

88.　　Fink, G. M. (1980). *Prelude to the presidency: The political character and legislative leadership style of Governor Jimmy Carter.* Westport, CT: Greenwood Press.

The book primarily focuses on the political character and legislative style that Carter exhibited while governor of Georgia between 1970 and 1974. It describes and analyzes Carter's often volatile political relations and his style of legislative leadership.

89.　　Fink, G. M., & Graham, H. D. (Eds.). (1998). *The Carter presidency:*

Policy choices in the post-New Deal era. Lawrence: University Press of Kansas.

This book uses the Carter administration as a case study to examine the New Deal's demise in a new age of limited government, monetarist fiscal policies, and social conservatism.

90.   Garrison, J. A. (1999). *Games advisors play: Foreign policy in the Nixon and Carter administrations.* College Station: Texas A&M University Press.

Examines case studies of foreign policy in the Nixon and Carter administrations. Specifically, it addresses how and why advisers manipulate the group process, under what conditions advisers engage in power games, and in what situations they are most effective in influencing presidential policy choices.

91.   Gaver, J. R. (1977). *The faith of Jimmy Carter.* New York: Manor Books.

Demonstrates how much faith others have in Jimmy Carter and his faith as a Christian, a president, and a human being.

92.   Glad, B. (1980). *Jimmy Carter, in search of the great White House.* New York: W. W. Norton.

This book examines President Carter's personality and character, tracing them from his childhood and early life to his political career in Georgia and beyond.

93.   Gleysteen, W. H., Jr. (1999). *Massive entanglement, marginal influence: Carter and Korea in crisis.* Washington, D.C.: Brookings Institution Press.

The author, former U.S. ambassador to Korea, examines how President Jimmy Carter's troop withdrawal and human rights policies—conceived in abstraction from East Asian realities—contributed to the assassination of Korean president Park Chung Hee.

94.   Godden, J. H. (1980). *Carter: The will to win.* Cincinnati, OH: Mosaic Press.

This is a condensed life story of Jimmy Carter up to the time he took political office.

95.   Grover, W. F. (1989). *The president as prisoner: A structural critique of the Carter and Reagan years.* Albany: State University of New York Press.

This book uses controversies over the Occupational Safety and Health Administration and the MX missile as examples of the power of a U.S. president. It argues, in part, that the limitations on power are economic and statist.

96.   Haas, G. A. (1992). *Jimmy Carter and the politics of frustration.* Jefferson, NC: McFarland.

This book describes how Jimmy Carter, a virtually unknown peanut processor from rural Plains, Georgia, ended up in the White House; how he comported himself in his newfound role as leader of the most powerful nation in the free world; and why, in the end, he was unable to succeed himself in office.

97.   Hargrove, E. C. (1988). *Jimmy Carter as president: Leadership and the politics of the public good.* Baton Rouge: Louisiana State University Press.

This book concentrates on Jimmy Carter's management of policy within his administration and his style as a decision maker. It portrays Carter's political personality; explores his handling of the different areas of domestic, economic, and foreign policy-making processes; and assesses his effectiveness as president by matching his skills and strategies of leadership to his historical opportunities.

98.   Hefley, J. C., & Hefley, M. (1977). *The church that produced a president.* New York: Wyden Books.

Examines Jimmy Carter's religious background, his church, and his aspirations to be God's man in a secular world of politics.

99.   Hurst, S. (1996). *The Carter administration and Vietnam.* New York: St. Martin's Press.

The book focuses on the attempt of the Carter administration to normalize relations with Vietnam and the reasons for the failure of that effort. Using a belief systems approach to explain the policy choices of key decision makers, the book presents a new explanation of the policy in question and of the decision to abandon the attempt to normalize relations at the end of 1978.

100.   Hyatt, R. (1977). *The Carters of Plains.* Hunstville, AL: Strode.

This book traces Jimmy Carter's steps through two years of campaigning and looks at the southern Georgia region that spawned him.

101.   Isaacs, H. (1977). *Jimmy Carter's peanut brigade*. Dallas, TX: Taylor.

        The author writes about supporters and volunteers—known as the "Pea-
        nut Brigade"—who worked tirelessly on Carter's campaign to ensure that
        he was elected U.S. president.

102.   Jones, C. O. (1988). *The trusteeship presidency: Jimmy Carter and the
        United States Congress*. Baton Rouge: Louisiana State University Press.

        Offers an interpretation and explanation of Carter's presidential policy.
        Focuses on the special political conditions associated with the Carter presi-
        dency and the trusteeship interpretation of his role that influenced the
        president's relationship with Congress between 1977 and 1980.

103.   Jordan, H. (1982). *Crisis: The last year of the Carter presidency*. New
        York: G. P. Putnam.

        The author, former chief adviser to President Jimmy Carter, provides a
        narrative of the final year of the Carter presidency, which featured in
        particular the American hostage situation in Iran and his failed reelection
        bid.

104.   Kaufman, B. I. (1993). *The presidency of James Earl Carter, Jr*. Lawrence:
        University Press of Kansas.

        The author takes the position that Carter failed to establish the base of
        public support and political legitimacy that he needed in order to be suc-
        cessful in his role as a trustee president.

105.   Kucharsky, D. (1976). *The man from Plains: The mind and spirit of Jimmy
        Carter*. New York: Harper & Row.

        This book unravels the mysteries of Carter's extraordinary success story
        as he emerged from Jimmy who? to the nominee of the 1976 Democratic
        National Convention and evaluates the man and his thinking.

106.   Lake, A. (1985). *Third World radical regimes: U.S. policy under Carter
        and Reagan*. New York: Foreign Policy Association.

        Using the Carter and Reagan administrations as case studies, this book
        examines questions and policies about the fundamental goals and values
        that the United States should pursue when facing the challenges posed by
        Third World revolutions.

107.   Lance, B. (1991). *The truth of the matter: My life in and out of politics.* New York: Summit Books.

       The former cabinet-level official in the Carter administration writes about his experiences and tenure in the government.

108.   Lankevich, G. J. (Ed.). (1981). *James E. Carter, 1924: Chronology—documents—bibliographical aids.* Dobbs Ferry, NY: Oceana.

       This volume chronicles the life and career of Jimmy Carter, from his hometown Plains, Georgia, to the White House in Washington, D.C. It also contains key documents about his presidency and important speeches that he made during his tenure.

109.   Lasky, V. (1979). *Jimmy Carter: The man and the myth.* New York: Richard Marek.

       The book critically examines Carter's presidency, arguing that although he rode into office because of the Watergate scandal, he was also its victim and that he failed to perform to the expectations of the American people.

110.   Lynn, L. E., Jr., & Whitman, D. DeF. (1981). *The president as policymaker: Jimmy Carter and welfare reform.* Philadelphia: Temple University Press.

       Examines the role of President Jimmy Carter in the development of a welfare reform package for America. It describes Carter's leadership within his own administration, then evaluates this experience by comparing it with the experiences of other presidents.

111.   Maddox, R. L. (1984). *Preacher at the White House.* Nashville, TN: Broadman Press.

       Examines the spiritual life of Jimmy Carter, noting that the Carter years will go down in American history books as an era of resurgent, intense involvement by religious groups in politics, particularly the conservative community.

112.   Maga, T. P., & Katsaros, T. (Eds.). (1994). *The world of Jimmy Carter: U.S. foreign policy 1977–81.* West Haven, CT: University of New Haven Press.

       Using archival research and oral interviews, the book examines the rea-

sons behind Carter's "call" to duty and why the international community
has respected his foreign policy both during and after his presidency.

113.   Maloney, W. E. (1977). *The Jimmy Carter dictionary: How to under-
        stand your president and speak southern.* Chicago: Playboy Press.

        This is a humorous book showing dozens of never seen-before pictures,
        including Carter at home, on the campaign stump, and at the White House.

114.   Mazlish, B., & Diamond, E. (1979). *Jimmy Carter: A character portrait.*
        New York: Simon & Schuster.

        Provides an interpretive study of Carter's character and presidency and
        attempts to find what fires his spirit and what dampens it.

115.   McMorrow, F. (1976). *Jimmy: The candidacy of Carter.* New York: Whirl-
        wind Book Co.

        The author chronicles Carter's rise from obscurity to the national front
        pages and into the White House.

116.   Meyer, P. (1978). *James Earl Carter: The man and the myth.* Kansas
        City, MO: Andrews & McMeel.

        This book examines Carter's personality and political actions in light of
        his campaign promise to Americans never to lie to them or tamper with
        the truth.

117.   Moens, A. (1990). *Foreign policy under Carter: Testing multiple advo-
        cacy decisions making.* Boulder, CO: Westview Press.

        This book offers an in-depth analysis of Carter's foreign policy decision-
        making process by means of a highly specialized model called "multiple
        advocacy."

118.   Mollenhoff, C. R. (1980). *The president who failed: Carter out of con-
        trol.* New York: Macmillan.

        This book primarily analyzes Carter's performance as president of the
        United States, arguing that during his tenure he made some compromises
        and accommodations without understanding the full implications of those
        actions. It alleges that Carter has tried to hide the embarrassing details of
        faulty decisions and has drifted into the dangerous rhetoric of self-decep-
        tion and cover-up.

119.   Morris, K. E. (1996). *Jimmy Carter, American moralist: The life story and moral legacy of our thirty-ninth president.* Athens: University of Georgia Press.

In the first full-scale biography of America's 39th president since 1980, Morris shows readers that any conclusions about Carter's leadership and his handling of challenges as a president cannot ignore the moral quandary that vexed the nation.

120.   Mower, A. G., Jr. (1987). *Human rights and American foreign policy: The Carter and Reagan experience.* Westport, CT: Greenwood Press.

This book provides a comparison of the human rights concepts, objectives, and policies of the Carter and Reagan administrations. The comparison is developed through a general survey of these policies, a reliance on extensive interviewing and congressional hearings, and four case studies involving South Africa, Chile, South Korea, and the Soviet Union.

121.   Muravchik, J. (1986). *The uncertain crusade: Jimmy Carter and the dilemmas of human rights policy.* Lanham, MD: Hamilton Press.

This book reviews the history of Carter's human rights policy, focusing on its origins, its personnel, its goals, and its actions. It also explicates the critical dilemmas of the U.S. human rights policy, the ways that the Carter administration responded to them, and possible alternative responses.

122.   Neuringer, S. M. (1993). *The Carter administration, human rights, and the agony of Cambodia.* Lewiston, NY: Edwin Mellen Press.

This book, the first specialized case study of the Carter administration's response to the tragic developments in Cambodia, examines the complex interplay of factors that shaped American policy toward that Far Eastern country.

123.   Neyland, J. (1977). *The Carter family scrapbook: An intimate close-up of America's first family.* New York: Grosset & Dunlap.

After a personal visit with the Carters of Plains, Georgia, the author provides a firsthand glimpse into the first family.

124.   Nielsen, N. C. (1977). *The religion of President Carter.* Nashville, TN: Thomas Nelson.

This book, in part, looks at Jimmy Carter's religion, the circumstances surrounding his election as U.S. president, and his stance on race and international relations.

125.   Norton, H., & Slosser, B. (1976). *The miracle of Jimmy Carter*. Plainfield, NJ: Logos International.

This book sheds light on the former governor of Georgia, Jimmy Carter, as well as on his spiritual life and his temporal background, which may have worked together to take him to the White House.

126.   Orman, J. M. (1987). *Comparing presidential behavior: Carter, Reagan, and the macho presidential style*. Westport, CT: Greenwood Press.

This book compares Ronald Reagan's presidential leadership during his first term with Jimmy Carter's exercise of presidential power. Specifically, it evaluates the key presidential myth that keeps the presidential system going, the so-called macho presidential style.

127.   Pippert, W. G. (1978). *The spiritual journey of Jimmy Carter: In his own words*. New York: Macmillan.

This book attempts to convey to the American public Jimmy Carter's belief and faith in Christ by presenting his words exactly as he used them in his public speeches and statements.

128.   Powell, J. (1984). *The other side of the story*. New York: William Morrow.

The author, press secretary in the Carter administration, provides insight into, and his own personal feelings about, how the American media covered the administration.

129.   Poynter, M. (1978). *The Jimmy Carter story*. New York: Julian Messner.

Illustrated with photographs, this book depicts the life and public career of President Jimmy Carter.

130.   *Public papers of the president of the United States: Jimmy Carter, 1977–1981*. Washington, D.C.: U.S. Government Printing Office.

This volume is part of several others that provide both a contemporary reference source and a permanent historical record of the 39th president of the United States, Jimmy Carter.

131.   Richardson, D. (Ed.). (1998). *Conversations with Carter*. Boulder, CO: Lynne Rienner.

This is a collection of interviews with Jimmy Carter in which he clarifies his public stands and private beliefs. The dialogue of these encounters demonstrates the growth of a principled man, coping with the major debates and concerns of the last quarter of the "American Century."

132.   Richman, D. A. (1989). *James E. Carter, 39th president of the United States*. Ada, OK: Garrett Educational Corp.

This book follows the life of Jimmy Carter, including his childhood, education, employment, political career, and term of the presidency.

133.   Rosati, J. A. (1987). *The Carter administration's quest for global community: Beliefs and their impact on behavior*. Columbia: University of South Carolina Press.

The author looks at the Carter administration's foreign policy from a political psychology perspective to explore how the role of beliefs may be used to advance the understanding of American foreign policy.

134.   Rosenbaum, H. D., & Ugrinsky, A. (Eds.). (1994). *The presidency and domestic policies of Jimmy Carter*. Westport, CT: Greenwood Press.

This book, based on the proceedings of the Carter Conference held at Hofstra University in New York, deals with Jimmy Carter's political history and emergence and with his management of domestic policies.

135.   Rosenbaum, H. D., & Ugrinsky, A. (Eds.). (1994). *Jimmy Carter: Foreign policy and post-presidential years*. Westport, CT: Greenwood Press.

This volume treats the entire scope of Carter's foreign policy. It also examines Carter's postpresidential career, arguing that an ex-president can shape the world without adopting either constitutional or legislative measures.

136.   Rozell, M. J. (1989). *The press and the Carter presidency*. Boulder, CO: Westview Press.

This book identifies and assesses the national journalistic evaluations of the Carter presidency. Specifically, it identifies and discusses the major themes in national press reporting and commentary on Jimmy Carter and his administration, from the latter stages to the 1976 campaign, through the conclusion of the 39th president's term in January 1981.

137.   Sandak, C. R. (1993). *The Carters*. New York: Crestwood Press.

Presents the life of Jimmy Carter, his family, and his years as the 39th American president.

138.   Schraff, A. (1998). *Jimmy Carter.* Springfield, NJ: Enslow.

This biography traces the early life of Jimmy Carter, his career in the navy, and his role as president and examines his postpresidential efforts in human rights and diplomacy.

139.   Schram, M. (1977). *Running for president 1976: The Carter campaign.* New York: Stein & Day.

Presents the story of Carter's rise from semiobscurity as an ex-governor of Georgia to the forefront of American politics as president.

140.   Seliktar, O. (2000). *Failing the crystal ball test: The Carter administration and the fundamentalist revolution in Iran.* Westport, CT: Praeger.

This book examines President Carter's application of new internationalism to Iran and suggests that Carter misread the likelihood of a fundamentalist takeover in Tehran.

141.   Shogan, R. (1977). *Promises to keep: Carter's first hundred days.* New York: Thomas Y. Crowell.

The author measures the expectations created by Carter's candidacy against the performance of his first 100 days in office and, in the process, illuminates the man. He places emphasis on the Carter administration's tone and direction, rather than on the substance of its policies and programs.

142.   Shoup, L. H. (1980). *The Carter presidency and beyond: Power and politics in the 1980's.* Palo Alto, CA: Ramparts Press.

The book examines not only the origins of the Carter presidency but also his administration's policies. It shows how these policies reflect the priorities of the corporate leaders who actually put Carter in office, not the constituency that voted for him.

143.   Skidmore, D. (1996). *Reversing course: Carter's foreign policy, domes-*

tic politics, and the failure of reform. Nashville, TN: Vanderbilt University Press.

This book primarily analyzes Carter's foreign policies.

144.   Smith, B. C. (1986). *Jimmy Carter, President.* New York: Walker.

Traces the life and career of the 39th U.S. president, describing his challenges, disappointments, and successes.

145.   Smith, B. S. (1977). *From peanuts to president.* Milwaukee, WI: Raintree Editions.

A biography, including timeline of Jimmy Carter, the farm boy from Georgia who became the 39th president of the United States.

146.   Smith, G. (1986). *Morality, reason, and power: American diplomacy in the Carter years.* New York: Hill & Wang.

This book examines American diplomacy during Carter's presidency, focusing primarily on how the administration confronted perennial themes and problems in international relations.

147.   Spear, J. (1995). *Carter and arms sales: Implementing the Carter administration's arms transfer restraint policy.* New York: Macmillan.

This book examines the origins, context, development, and fate of the Carter administration's conventional arms transfer restraint policy. It addresses such questions as: Why did the Carter administration's conventional arms transfer restraint policy fail? What can be learned from that failure?

148.   Spencer, D. S. (1988). *The Carter implosion: Jimmy Carter and the amateur style of diplomacy.* New York: Praeger.

This volume comprises a series of essays about the seemingly enormous gulf between the Carter administration's professed objectives and the tools that it was willing to employ to achieve them. It argues that Carter's campaign promise to inaugurate a new age of American greatness and to transform the world of sovereign nation-states was marred by his and his closest advisers' lack of political sophistication.

149.   St. John, J. (1976). *Jimmy Carter's betrayal of the South.* Ottawa, IL: Green Hill.

This book examines Carter's bid for the American presidency, arguing that his election to the White House would make a radical break with a long, conservative political tradition of the South.

150.   Strong, R. A. (1999). *Working in the world: Jimmy Carter and the making of American foreign policy.* Baton Rouge: Louisiana State University Press.

This book, based primarily on interviews with participants and on recently released documents in the Carter presidential library, examines how the 39th president of the United States addressed and accomplished the work of foreign policy.

151.   Stroud, K. (1977). *How Jimmy won: The victory campaign from Plains to the White House.* New York: William Morrow.

The book examines Carter's life from peanut farmer, to Georgia governor, to U.S. president, arguing that he won the White House because he offered the hope of something better and because of Watergate.

152.   Thomas, S. (1978). *Jimmy Carter: From peanuts to presidency.* Cornwall, Ontario, Canada: Vesta.

This book provides an appraisal of Jimmy Carter, noting that he diagnosed the disease of affluent America and introduced a moral dimension into politics to heal it.

153.   Thompson, K. W. (Ed.). (1990). *The Carter presidency: Fourteen intimate perspectives of Jimmy Carter (Portraits of American Presidents, Vol. 8).* Lanham, MD: University Press of America.

This volume builds an oral historical record of the Carter presidency, in particular, the Carter White House.

154.   Thornton, R. C. (1991). *The Carter years: Toward a new global order.* New York: Paragon House.

This volume examines continuity and change in American foreign policy during the Carter years. It argues that while the administration of Jimmy Carter came into office fully prepared to carry forward the general strategy of a new global order, a major Soviet strategic weapons breakthrough almost immediately forced its reconsideration.

155.   Troester, R. (1996). *Jimmy Carter as peacemaker: A post-presidential biography.* Westport, CT: Praeger.

This book demonstrates how the Carter postpresidency—after January 1981—has redefined the role of former presidents and refurbished Carter's image. It argues that Carter has shown that through active involvement in world affairs and humanitarian causes and through the careful invest-ment of postpresidential credibility and political capital, a former presi-dent can make significant contributions to a more peaceful, stable world.

156. Turner, R. L. (Ed.). (1976). *"I'll never lie to you": Jimmy Carter in his own words*. New York: Ballantine Books.

Full of quotations, this book assesses Carter's own words, including speeches, position papers, impromptu sermons, and offhand private re-marks.

157. Veale, F., Jr. (1977). *Carter, a son of Georgia*. Cairo, GA: Veale.

Contains the most candid photographs ever taken of Jimmy Carter as an early campaigner and as a "man of the people," revealing an astronomi-cal rise to the presidency.

158. Vincent, S. (Ed.). (1977). *Omens from the flight of birds: The 101 days of Jimmy Carter*. San Francisco: Momo's Press.

Through the use of poems, stories, diary entries, documents, cartoons, photographs, collages, and drawings, the contributors to this book reveal and illuminate the character and spirit of life with and under President Jimmy Carter.

159. Walker, B. J. (1977). *The picture life of Jimmy Carter*. New York: Franklin Watts.

Sheds some light on the man behind the smile, Jimmy Carter, places him in the context of southern politics, and looks at the forces that shaped his views as a southerner.

160. Walton, H. (1992). *The native son presidential candidate: The Carter vote in Georgia*. New York: Praeger.

Provides a longitudinal analysis of Georgia state voting in all of Jimmy Carter's campaign from his 1962 state Senate race to the 1980 presiden-tial contest. Specifically, it documents the electoral support that Carter received in his 12 elections in Georgia and the support that he garnered for his former vice president in the 1984 presidential election.

RONALD REAGAN

161. Abrams, H. L. (1993). *"The president has been shot": Confusion, disability, and the 25th Amendment in the aftermath of the attempted assassination of Ronald Reagan*. New York: W. W. Norton.

    The author draws implications from the first opportunity for invoking the disability provisions of the 25th Amendment to the U.S. Constitution since its ratification in 1967 following the assassination attempt on Ronald Reagan in March 1981.

162. Ackerman, F. (1982). *Reaganomics: Rhetoric vs. reality*. Boston: South End Press.

    This book is an explanation and critique of "Reaganomics." It is based on a decidedly unmagical view of the American economy and of the failings of both old and new styles of conservative policy.

163. Adler, B. (Ed.). (1985). *Ronnie and Nancy: A very special love story*. New York: Crown.

    This book tells the story of the romance between Ronald and Nancy Reagan, from Hollywood to the White House.

164. Adler, B. (Ed.). (1996). *The uncommon wisdom of Ronald Reagan: A portrait of his own words*. Boston: Little, Brown.

    This collection of quotations presents many of Reagan's anecdotes, speeches, writings, and off-the-cuff remarks. It is organized chronologically from his childhood to his presidency, including reflections on politics, himself, his family, and his country.

165. Adler, B., & Adler, B., Jr. (Eds.). (1998). *The Reagan wit: The humor of the American president*. New York: William Morrow.

    President Reagan's humor is presented in this collection of quotations, both famous and unfamiliar, which follows the former president from his youth to his adult years.

166. Amaker, N. C. (1988). *Civil rights and the Reagan administration*. Lanham, MD: University Press of America.

    Evaluates Reagan administration's record in education, federally assisted programs, housing, employment, and voting.

167.   Anderson, M. (1990). *Revolution: The Reagan legacy.* Stanford, CA: Hoover Institution Press.

This book is primarily a story about Ronald Reagan's rise to power in America. It tells what kind of man he is, the public policies that he thought were important, and the main consequences of these policies.

168.   Arca, E., & Pamel, G. J. (Eds.). (1984). *The triumph of the American spirit: The presidential speeches of Ronald Reagan.* Detroit: National Productions Corp.

This book contains the most significant of the many speeches that President Ronald Reagan made in the first term of his office.

169.   Arnson, C. J. (1989). *Crossroads: Congress, the Reagan administration, and Central America.* New York: Pantheon Books.

This book describes the struggle and confrontation between President Ronald Reagan and his critics in Congress over Central America policy in the 1980s.

170.   Aruri, N., Moughrabi, F., & Stork, J. (1983). *Reagan and the Middle East.* Belmont, MA: Association of Arab-American University Graduates.

Focuses on the policies of the Reagan administration with respect to the Arab–Israeli conflict.

171.   Barilleaux, R. J. (1988). *The post-modern presidency: The office after Ronald Reagan.* New York: Praeger.

Among other things, this book examines changes in the American political environment that affected the presidency, assesses the impact of Ronald Reagan on the office, and considers the implications of the postmodern presidency for future holders.

172.   Barrett, L. I. (1983). *Gambling with history: Ronald Reagan in the White House.* Garden City, NY: Doubleday.

The author uses interviews and observations to trace the origins of Reagan's political philosophy, his economic program, his arms control negotiations, and his relationships with his advisers and wife, Nancy.

173.   Bartlett, B. R. (1981). *Reaganomics: Supply side economics in action.* Westport, CT: Arlington House.

This book is an introduction to supply-side economics within which Reagan operated.

174.   Bell, C. (1989). *The Reagan paradox: American foreign policy in the 1980s.* Aldershot, Hants, UK: Edward Elgar.

This book analyzes U.S. foreign policy during the Reagan era, focusing primarily on such issues as U.S.–Soviet relations, the Atlantic alliance, and Third World conflicts.

175.   Berman, L. (Ed.). (1990). *Looking back on the Reagan presidency.* Baltimore: Johns Hopkins University Press.

This book is a collection of conference papers presented at the University of California, Davis, in May 1988 to review the Reagan administration's impact in four major areas: foreign policy, economic and fiscal policy, institutional changes, and electoral and congressional relations.

176.   Bjork, R. S. (1992). *The Strategic Defense Initiative: Symbolic containment of the nuclear threat.* Albany: State University of New York Press.

Analyzing linguistic strategies, the author studies the Reagan and Bush administrations' efforts in selling the Strategic Defense Initiative (SDI) program to U.S. Congress and the American public. The book shows how the SDI program appealed symbolically to the nostalgic sense of American history, replete with powerful images of American innocence and technological ingenuity in the face of difficult obstacles.

177.   Block, H. (1984). *Herblock through the looking glass: The Reagan years in words and pictures.* New York: W. W. Norton.

America's foremost cartoon commentator paints a picture of words and pictures about the Reagan years and their effects on history, politics, and on the lives of Americans.

178.   Blumenthal, S., & Edsall, T. B. (Eds.). (1988). *The Reagan legacy.* New York: Pantheon Books.

The seven contributors to this book evaluate the Reagan legacy in terms of its impact on politics, economics, diplomacy, law, culture, and ideology.

179.   Boaz, D. (Ed.). (1988). *Assessing the Reagan years.* Washington, D.C.: Cato Institute Press.

The essays in this volume examine Reagan administration's policies and actions, from education, foreign aid, judges' selection, international relations, to antitrust laws.

180. Bosch, A. (2000). *Reagan: An American story.* New York: TV Books.

The author uses his connection to the advisers and family of Ronald Reagan to examine the former president from his midwestern childhood, through his acting career and political careers in California and the White House, to his life in retirement.

181. Boskin, M. J. (1989). *Reagan and the economy: The successes, failures and unfinished agenda.* San Francisco: ICS Press. (Institute for Contemporary Studies Press).

This book critiques the Reagan administration's economic policies.

182. Boyarsky, B. (1981). *Ronald Reagan: His life and rise to the presidency.* New York: Random House.

This book focuses on the two terms of Reagan's governorship in California, analyzing his strengths and weaknesses as a leader and how these qualities would impact his role as the 40th president of the United States.

183. Boyer, P. (Ed.). (1990). *Reagan as president: Contemporary views of the man, his politics, and his policies.* Chicago: Ivan R. Dee.

This book not only explores domestic programs and foreign policies under Reagan but also examines the man himself. It presents a careful selection of almost 100 articles, editorials, and essays written between 1980 and 1989 by journalists and commentators unfolding the Reagan presidency's policies, ideology, style, and Reagan the man.

184. Brown, E. G. (1970). *Reagan and reality: The two Californias.* New York: Praeger.

This book examines the record of Ronald Reagan as governor of California, how his governorship fits into the contemporary pattern of politics in the state, and what it could mean to the rest of the nation.

185. Brown, E. G., & Brown, B. (1976). *Reagan, the political chameleon.* New York: Praeger.

This book deals with Reagan's promises to America versus the reality of his accomplishments as governor of California and his early days of campaigning for the presidency.

186.   Brown, J. M. (1995). *Explaining the Reagan years in Central America: A world system perspective.* Lanham, MD: University Press of America.

The author analyzes the relationship between the United States and Central America and traces Central America's origins as a collection of colonies on the periphery of the world system, through eras of expansionism, imperialism, world wars, and triumph as global hegemony, and into ultimate crisis, decline, and conservative reaction through the 1980s.

187.   Brownstein, R., & Easton, N. (1982). *Reagan's ruling class: Portraits of the president's top one hundred officials.* New York: Pantheon Books.

Profiles appointees in the executive branch of the Reagan administration.

188.   Brune, L. H. (1991). *Chronological history of U.S. foreign relations, January 21, 1981 to January 20, 1989: The Reagan years, Vol. 3.* New York: Garland.

Arranged chronologically, this volume focuses on American foreign relations, and economy and trade, as well as national security and political matters.

189.   Busby, R. (1999). *Reagan and the Iran–Contra Affair: The politics of presidential recovery.* New York: Macmillan.

This book examines the efforts of the Reagan administration to recover its public credibility in the 12 months following the exposure of the Iran–Contra scandal of late 1986 and 1987. Using comparative analysis, it explores the impact of the scandal upon the presidential office, the problems that confronted President Reagan during the whole affair, and the centrality of damage-control efforts to the well-being of the modern presidency.

190.   Campagna, A. S. (1994). *The economy in the Reagan years: The economic consequences of the Reagan administrations.* Westport, CT: Greenwood Press.

This book conducts elaborate research on Reagan administration policies, describing what was planned by the government, what actually happened, and what has been left for the future to deal with.

191.   Cannon, L. (1982). *Reagan*. New York: G. P. Putnam.

This book is about Ronald Reagan, his early years, his rise to the presidency, and his first year in the White House. It also is a book about politics and about the American political arenas in which Reagan competed.

192.   Cannon, L. (1991). *President Reagan: The role of a lifetime*. New York: Simon & Schuster.

This book is an effort by the author to write about Reagan as he truly was. Focusing on his performance in the presidency while also examining his life, the author draws upon scores of interviews with Reagan, his former aides, advisers, friends, scholars, and critics, as well as his own journalistic writings as senior White House correspondent for the *Washington Post*.

193.   Cardigan, J. H. (1995). *Ronald Reagan: A remarkable life*. Kansas City, MO: Andrews & McMeel.

This book, filled with color and black-and-white pictures, chronicles the life of Ronald Reagan, from his early years, to his success as a film star, to his ascent to the presidency and his current retirement.

194.   Carothers, T. (1991). *In the name of democracy: U.S. policy toward Latin America in the Reagan years*. Los Angeles: University of California Press.

Traces the evolution of the Reagan administration's policy toward Latin America.

195.   Carter, H. (1988). *The Reagan years*. New York: George Braziller.

This book contains chronologically and thematically arranged columns written by the author for the *Wall Street Journal* between the late 1980 and mid-1988 assessing the Reagan years.

196.   Celmer, M. A. (1987). *Terrorism, U.S. strategy, and Reagan policies*. Westport, CT: Greenwood Press.

Traces the evolution of U.S. policy and antiterrorism bureaucracy and command structure from the establishment by President Richard Nixon of the Cabinet Committee to combat terrorism, to President Reagan's signing of National Security Decision Directive 138, sanctioning the use of more aggressive counterterrorist actions, such as the U.S. raid on Libya.

197.   Churba, J. (1984). *The American retreat: The Reagan foreign and defense policy*. Chicago: Regnery Gateway.

Examines the rationale for the Soviet Union's campaign for world hegemony, the shape of the plan initiated in 1975 for its implementation, and the measures that must be taken to protect the interests of the United States and the rest of the free world.

198.   Cohen, W. S., & Mitchell, G. J. (1988). *Men of zeal: A candid inside story of the Iran–Contra hearings*. New York: Viking Books.

The authors of this book, both U.S. senators, describe their observations and reflections of the Iran–Contra affair, which surfaced during the Reagan years.

199.   Combs, J. (1993). *The Reagan range: The nostalgic myth in American politics*. Bowling Green, OH: Bowling Green State University Popular Press.

This book links Ronald Reagan to American popular mythology. It argues that Reagan's political success can be understood, in part, by seeing him as part of the revivified nostalgic myth that so informs and shapes American political life, of which he was the latest successful representative.

200.   Congressional Quarterly (CQ). (1981). *President Reagan*. Washington, D.C.: Author.

This book offers a thorough introduction to the 40th president of the United States—the man, his philosophy, and his record.

201.   *The cumulated indexes to the public papers of the president of the United States, Ronald Reagan, 1981–1989*. (1995). Lanham, MD: Bernan Press.

The collected indexes in this book make it simple to search through the many volumes of presidential papers for each particular person, subject, or category of document during the Reagan presidency.

202.   Dallek, M. (2000). *The right moment: Ronald Reagan's first victory and the decisive turning point in American politics*. New York: Free Press.

The author examines the Reagan revolution which started in the early and mid-1960s with his defeat of two-term incumbent California governor Edmund "Pat" Brown and his quest for a new social order for America.

203. Dallek, R. (1984). *Ronald Reagan: The politics of symbolism.* Cambridge: Harvard University Press.

Presents a detailed portrait of Reagan and his politics, from his childhood years through the California governorship, to the first years of the presidency. The book helps broaden and deepen our understanding of the Reagan phenomenon in American life.

204. Damm, H. von. (Ed.). (1976). *Sincerely, Ronald Reagan.* Ottawa, IL: Green Hill.

The author, one of the most influential women in the Reagan administration, who later become U.S. ambassador to her native Austria, writes about her life and rise to the top as Reagan's personal secretary and then the director of presidential personnel.

205. Davis, P. (1992). *The way I see it.* New York: G. P. Putnam.

The daughter of Ronald and Nancy Reagan provides behind-the-doors account of the Reagan household and about her experiences and troubled past as part of America's first family.

206. Deaver, M. K. (2001). *A different drummer: My thirty years with Ronald Reagan: An American hero.* New York: HarperCollins. The longtime friend and former aide of Ronald Reagan paints a portrait of his experiences and memories of the former president.

207. Deaver, M. K. (With Mickey Herskowitz). (1988). *Behind the scenes: In which the author talks about Ronald & Nancy & himself.* New York: William Morrow.

This is a memoir of a former White House official who fell out of favor with the Reagans and made several allegations against the administration.

208. DeMause, L. (1984). *Reagan's America.* New York: Creative Roots.

Using thousands of documents, including cartoons, pictures, news headlines, and magazine covers, the author tells a story about the feelings and fantasies that Americans shared in Reagan's America.

209. Denton, J. S., & Schweizer, P. (Eds.). (1988). *Grinning with the gipper: The wit, wisdom, and wisecracks of Ronald Reagan.* New York: Atlantic Monthly Press.

This book tells the story and paints a self-portrait of Reagan's masterful use of humor in his public speeches and utterances.

210.   Denton, R. E., Jr. (1988). *The primetime presidency of Ronald Reagan: The era of the television presidency.* New York: Praeger.

This book is about the rhetorical dimensions of the American presidency, focusing primarily on Ronald Reagan, affectionately labeled as "the Great Communicator." It looks at three levels of interaction involving the presidency: the interaction of the office with the general public, the interaction of the office with specific individuals, and the interaction of the office with officeholders.

211.   Devaney, J. (1990). *Ronald Reagan, President.* New York: Walker.

This biographic book is illustrated with many pictures from Ronald Reagan's early years.

212.   Devine, D. J. (1983). *Reagan electionomics: How Reagan ambushed the pollsters.* Ottawa, IL: Green Hill.

This book argues that the "Reagan revolution" occurred because of three underlying realities: American politics is dynamic; the American people are generally conservative; it served as a conservative movement catalyst. It uses political science tools to understand reality, to predict it, to help shape a rational strategy to deal with it, and to win elections with it.

213.   D'Souza, D. (1997). *Ronald Reagan: How an ordinary man became an extraordinary leader.* New York: Simon & Schuster.

This book shows how Ronald Reagan, a man of distinctive personality, was able to transform the political landscape in a way that made a permanent impact on America and the rest of the world.

214.   Dugger, R. (1983). *On Reagan: The man and his presidency.* New York: McGraw-Hill.

This book attempts to help us understand Ronald Reagan and his administration, focusing on his policies as the 40th president of the United States.

215.   Durant, R. F. (1992). *The administrative presidency revisited: Public lands, the BLM, and the Reagan revolution.* Albany: State University of New York Press.

The primary focus of this book is President Ronald Reagan's efforts to reorient natural resource policy in the Bureau of Land Management (BLM) in New Mexico.

216.   Edwards, A. (1987). *Early Reagan: The rise to power*. New York: William Morrow.

The book provides a narrative of the first 55 years of Ronald Reagan's life, chronicling important events and actions.

217.   Edwards, L. (1981). *Ronald Reagan: A political biography*. Houston, TX: Norland.

This book looks at the total life of Ronald Reagan, emphasizing his special talents as a rhetorician and reveals how and why he won against formidable odds—and what kind of president he would be.

218.   Erickson, P. D. (1985). *Reagan speaks: The making of an American myth*. New York: New York University Press.

Examines President Reagan's techniques as a teller of tales who captured the hearts and imaginations of a majority of the American electorate in the first half of the 1980s through the skillful use of what may be either "idealistic inspiration or cynical manipulation." It deals as strictly as possible with the textual evidence of Ronald Reagan's ideas and feelings about the American people.

219.   Evans, R., & Novak, R. (1981). *The Reagan revolution*. New York: E. P. Dutton.

Describes the origins, purposes, and prospects of "the Reagan revolution"—tax, budget, and regulatory reforms, as well as tough foreign and military policy and moral majority social issues.

220.   Fischer, B. A. (1997). *The Reagan reversal: Foreign policy and the end of the Cold War*. Columbia: University of Missouri Press.

This book challenges the conventional wisdom about President Reagan and reveals that he was the driving force behind U.S.–Soviet policy.

221.   Fitzgerald, F. (2000). *Way out there in the blue: Reagan, Star Wars and the end of the Cold War*. New York: Simon & Schuster.

This book is part Reagan biography and part analysis of his Strategic Defense Initiative (SDI), an impenetrable shield located in space that would destroy any nuclear missiles launched at the United States. The book also looks at the Iran arms-for-hostage crisis, the Iran–Contra scandals, and Reagan's arms-control talks with Russian leader Mikhail Gorbachev.

222.   Fox, M. V. (1986). *Mr. President: The story of Ronald Reagan*. Rev. ed. Hillside, NJ: Enslow.

Traces Ronald Reagan's life, from his boyhood days in small midwestern towns, through his successful careers as sportscaster, Hollywood scene actor, and finally politician and statesman.

223.   Friedman, B. (1988). *Day of reckoning: The consequences of American economic policy under Reagan and after*. New York: Random House.

This book argues that the American economic policy in the 1980s, leading to the running up of the national debt and selling off assets, would only lead to a lower standard of living for individual Americans and reduce American influence and importance in world affairs.

224.   Friedman, B. (1995). *Regulation in the Reagan–Bush era: The eruption of presidential influence*. Pittsburgh: University of Pittsburgh Press.

This is a comprehensive summary of the Reagan administration's effort to promote a conservative agenda through regulatory reform.

225.   Friedman, S. P. (1986). *Ronald Reagan: His life story in pictures*. New York: Dodd, Mead.

The book covers in photographs and text all the important events of Ronald Reagan's life.

226.   Gallick, S. (1999). *Ronald Reagan: The pictorial biography*. Philadelphia: Courage Books.

The story in this book follows the life of Reagan, from his modest midwestern beginnings, through his successful Hollywood career, to his two-term tenure in the White House. Illustrated with 130 full-color and black-and-white photographs, this pictorial biography celebrates the life, achievements, and legacy of Ronald Reagan.

227.   Gardner, G. (1981). *The actor, a photographic interview with Ronald Reagan*. New York: Pocket Books.

The author uses pictures to depict the man who used his talent to become the 40th president of the United States.

228.   Gartner, A., Greer, C., & Riessman, F. (Eds.). (1981). *What Reagan is doing to us*. New York: Harper & Row.

This book provides a map of the Reagan administration's domestic and foreign policies during its first year in office. Specifically, it discusses the effect of Reagan's policies on the economy, foreign policy, women, minorities, neighborhoods, crime, health, education, and welfare.

229.   Gergen, D. R. (2000). *Eyewitness to power: The essence of leadership, Nixon to Clinton*. New York: Simon & Schuster.

The author, an adviser to Presidents Nixon, Ford, Reagan, and Clinton, offers insights into the strengths and weaknesses of their administrations and draws from them lessons for future leaders.

230.   Germond, J. W., & Witcover, J. (1981). *Blue smoke and mirrors: How Reagan won and why Carter lost the election of 1980*. New York: Viking Press.

Chronicles and examines the turning points in the 1980 U.S. presidential election and how they contributed to the landslide victory of Ronald Reagan over Jimmy Carter.

231.   Giuliano, G. (1999). *Ronald Reagan: A tribute*. New York: Random House.

This is a collection of Reagan's most memorable speeches, public addresses, and debates. It pays glowing tribute to one of America's best-loved icons and leaders.

232.   Givel, M. (1990). *The War on Poverty revisited: The Community Services Block Grant program in the Reagan years*. Lanham, MD: University Press of America.

Focuses on the new Community Services Block Grant program, which was administered under the centralized categorical format by the U.S. Office of Economic Opportunity from 1964 to 1973 and the U.S. Community Services Administration from 1974 to 1980.

233.   Goldstein, W. (Ed.). (1986). *Reagan's leadership and the Atlantic alliance: Views from Europe and America*. Washington, D.C.: Pergamon-Bassey's International Defence Publishers.

This book resulted from the 13th annual meeting of the Standing Conference of Atlantic Organizations (SCAO) in Racine, Wisconsin, in July 1985, at which it examined the likely thrust of U.S. foreign policy in the second term of President Reagan's administration.

234.   Goodman, M. R., & Wrightson, M. T. (1987). *Managing regulatory reform: The Reagan strategy and its impact*. New York: Praeger.

Based on several case studies from different policy areas, this book assesses the success and the problems caused by Reagan's avowed "new federalism" approach through intergovernmental regulatory relief. It discusses in detail such issues as intergovernmental relations, nuclear energy policy, and environmental policy.

235.   Green, M., & MacColl, G. (1983). *There he goes again: Ronald Reagan's reign of error*. New York: Pantheon Books.

Focuses on six kinds of alleged errors during Reagan's presidency: obvious exaggerations, material omissions, contrived anecdotes, voodoo statistics, denials of unpleasant facts, and flat untruths.

236.   Greenhaw, W. (1982). *Elephants in the cottonfields: Ronald Reagan and the new Republican South*. New York: Macmillan.

This book offers insight into the rise and political operations of the Republican South, linking the party's future to the new conservative Republicanism spearheaded by President Ronald Reagan.

237.   Greenstein, F. I. (Ed.). (1983). *The Reagan presidency: An early assessment*. Baltimore: Johns Hopkins University Press.

The book provides early appraisal of the Reagan presidency, with attention to both its principal policies and strategy.

238.   Haftendorn, H., & Schissler, J. (Eds.). (1989). *The Reagan administration: A reconstruction of American strength*. Berlin, Germany: Walter de Gruyter.

This volume presents research on the domestic foundations of the Reagan administration's foreign, economic, and security policies.

239.   Hagstrom, J. (1988). *Beyond Reagan: The new landscape of American politics*. New York: W. W. Norton.

This book examines how America, from coast to coast, has fared during the Reagan era, how some politicians helped him achieve his goals, and how others fought hard to keep his most radical proposals from being enacted.

240.   Haig, A. M., Jr. (1984). *Caveat: Realism, Reagan and foreign policy.* New York: Macmillan.

This is the personal memoir of the U.S. secretary of state in the Reagan administration, describing events that happened in his incumbency.

241.   Hannaford, P. (1983). *The Reagans: A political portrait.* New York: Coward-McCann.

This is a biography of the Reagans, focusing on his public life, which was marked by the intense loyalty of those around him.

242.   Hannaford, P. (1999). *The quotable Ronald Reagan: The best of the great communicator, from A to Z.* Washington, D.C.: Regnery.

This book contains more than 600 memorable quotations of Ronald Reagan covering a wide variety of topics. These quotations capture the essence of Reagan's personality, wit, and charm—demonstrating why he was called the "Great Communicator."

243.   Hannaford, P. (Ed.). (1997). *Recollections of Reagan: A portrait of Ronald Reagan.* New York: William Morrow.

This book examines Reagan's early days in film, his election as governor of California, his unsuccessful bid for the White House in 1976, and his two-term presidency.

244.   Hannaford, P., & Hobbs, C. D. (1994). *Remembering Reagan.* Washington, D.C.: Regnery.

This is a pictorial record of the high points—and the low—of Ronald Reagan's White House years, as seen through the lenses of White House photographers.

245.   Hertsgaard, M. (1988). *On bended knee: The press and the Reagan presidency.* New York: Farrar, Straus, & Giroux.

Using interviews and analysis of hundreds of newspaper articles and television stories, the author tells the story of the relationship between the press and the White House during the Reagan years.

246.   Hill, D. M., Moore, R. A., & Williams, P. (1990). *The Reagan presidency: An incomplete revolution?* New York: Macmillan.

This book explores the Reagan policy style and substance, considers the initial aspirations of the two Reagan administrations, examines the constraints with which they had to contend, and assesses the legacy of achievement and failure.

247.   Hirschmann, D. (1989). *Changing attitudes of black South Africans toward the United States.* Lewiston, NY: Edwin Mellen Press.

Using in-depth interviews, the author analyzes the impact that the Reagan presidency had and is still having on the attitudes of black South Africans toward Americans in general and the United States in particular.

248.   Hobbs, C. D. (1976). *Ronald Reagan's call to action.* Nashville, TN: Thomas Nelson.

This book presents Ronald Reagan's political philosophy as he presented it to the author in a series of taped interviews in the spring and early summer of 1975. Reagan's position was that government is the problem, not the solution, in combating recession, inflation, unemployment, and other ills plaguing America.

249.   Hogan, J. (Ed.). (1990). *The Reagan years: The record in presidential leadership.* Manchester, UK: Manchester University Press.

Examines the record of the Reagan presidency in both managing the institutions of the federal government and in achieving desired changes in prevailing domestic and foreign policies.

250.   Houck, D. W., & Kiewe, A. (Eds.). (1993). *Actor, ideologue, politician: The public speeches of Ronald Reagan.* Westport, CT: Greenwood Press.

This is a collection of President Reagan's public speeches during all phases of his political life.

251.   Hyland, W. G. (Ed.). (1981). *The Reagan foreign policy.* New York: Meridian.

The contributors to this volume examine how U.S. foreign policy has played out in the Middle East, Central America, Africa, and other hot spots around the world. Also they discuss the Reagan administration's struggle with Congress for control of foreign policy and the possible repercussions of the Iran–Contra affair.

252.   Israel, F. L. (1987). *Ronald Reagan's weekly radio addresses: The president speaks to America: Volume 1: The first term.* Wilmington, DE: Scholarly Resources.

This is a collection of 125 transcripts of weekly radio broadcasts by President Ronald Reagan conveying his thoughts on essential national issues and his philosophy to the American public.

253.   Jeffords, S. (1993). *Hard bodies: Hollywood masculinity in the Reagan era.* New Brunswick, NJ: Rutgers University Press.

This book looks at some of the most popular films of the Reagan era and examines how the characters, themes, and stories presented in them often helped to reinforce and disseminate the policies, programs, and beliefs of the "Reagan revolution." The movies include *Rambo, Lethal Weapon, Die Hard, Robocop, Back to the Future, Star Wars, the Indiana Jones series, Mississippi Burning, Rain Man, Batman*, and *Unforgiven.*

254.   Jentleson, B. W. (1995). *With friends like these: Reagan, Bush, and Saddam, 1982–1990.* New York: W. W. Norton.

The book analyzes the Reagan–Bush strategy of bringing Iraqi president Saddam Hussein into the family of nations and provides an account of the politics, processes, and consequences of U.S. policy toward Iraq. It examines how the policy was pursued, why it failed, and what lessons can be derived.

255.   Jinks, H. (1986). *Ronald Reagan—smile, style, and guile.* New York: Vantage Press.

The author uses the research of many popular and experienced commentators to point out certain pluses and minuses in American government, specifically during the presidency of Ronald Reagan.

256.   Johnson, H. (1992). *Sleepwalking through history: America in the Reagan years.* New York: Anchor Books.

The book argues that despite America's economic and military power, as well as abundant natural and human resources, several problems threaten the country's standing and continued prosperity in the 1990s. It concludes, for example, that if America falls, it will likely be from internal causes: failure to address long-festering social and economic problems, subversion of its constitutional systems, the corruption and ineffectiveness of its government, and cynicism and inattention of its people.

257.   Jorstad, E. (1981). *Evangelicals in the White House: The cultural maturation of born-again Christians.* Lewiston, NY: Edwin Mellen Press.

This book distinguishes between moderate, "press-on" Jimmy Carter and conservative "hold-fast" Ronald Reagan, attributing Reagan's and the "hold-fast" evangelicals' political successes to their mastery of computer and television technology.

258.   Joseph, J. W. (1993). *Between realism and reality: The Reagan administration and international debt.* Lanham, MD: University Press of America.

This book primarily examines the Reagan administration's policy regarding international debt between 1981 and 1985.

259.   Judson, K. (1997). *Ronald Reagan.* Springfield, NJ: Enslow.

The book traces the life and career of former President Ronald Reagan, from his childhood in Illinois, through his time as an actor, to his activities in public office.

260.   Kiewe, A., & Houck, D. W. (1991). *A shining city on a hill: Ronald Reagan's economic rhetoric, 1951–1989.* New York: Praeger.

This book uses a variety of theoretical approaches to examine the verbal tactics used by Reagan over a 40-year period to sell his economic policies.

261.   Kirkpatrick, J. J. (1983). *The Reagan phenomenon and other speeches on foreign policy.* Washington, D.C.: American Enterprise Institute.

This book brings together selected speeches delivered by the author, former U.S. permanent representative to the United Nations and also to the cabinet and the National Security Council, on the foreign policy of the United States during the Reagan administration.

262.   Knelman, F. H. (1985). *Reagan, God, and the bomb: From myth to policy in the nuclear arms race.* Buffalo, NY: Prometheus Books.

This book attempts to supply evidence that the Reagan administration is the first since the end of World War II to make nuclear war fighting plans and to seek to destroy the Soviet Union.

263. Kozhimannil, V. T. (1989). *The Reagan presidency: Promises and performance: Awake America! Are you better off?* New York: Cimothas.

Examines Reagan's presidential policies on domestic and foreign issues, positing that the government not only must be made accountable and responsible to the people for its actions but also must serve the needs of the people.

264. Krepon, M. (1989). *Arms control in the Reagan administration: Volume 10.* Lanham, MD: University Press of America.

This is a collection of the author's analyses of arms control and the presidency, focusing on the Reagan administration.

265. Kurt, R., & Henry, D. (1992). *Ronald Reagan: The great communicator.* New York: Greenwood Press.

The authors trace the evolution of the union of political and religious rhetoric from its inception in Reagan's prepolitical years, through its fruition during his presidency. It provides a chronology of Reagan's major speeches, spanning more than 60 years (1928 to 1991), and an extensive bibliography of primary and secondary sources on Reagan as an orator.

266. Kyvig, D. E. (Ed.). (1990). *Reagan and the world.* Westport, CT: Greenwood Press.

This book's contributors, distinguished historians of international repute, discuss and assess the foreign relations policies and actions of the Reagan presidency with regard to the Soviet Union, East Asia, Latin America, the Middle East, Western Europe, and Africa.

267. Lagon, M. P. (1994). *The Reagan doctrine: Sources of American conduct in the Cold War's last chapter.* Westport, CT: Praeger.

This book examines Reagan's foreign policy doctrine of pledging aid to anti-Communist guerrillas in the Third World. The author applies two alternative explanations—notably, "realist" theory and "elite belief" theory—to test his study's assumptions and concludes that while each perspective is necessary to explain the Reagan doctrine, neither is sufficient by itself.

268.   Laham, N. (1998). *The Reagan presidency and the politics of race: In pursuit of colorblind justice and limited government.* Westport, CT: Greenwood Press.

The author analyzes the major initiatives that Reagan pursued trying to curb enforcement of civil rights laws in America by, first, prohibiting mandatory employer use of minority and white female hiring goals and, second, vetoing the Civil Rights Restoration Act.

269.   Laham, N. (2000). *Ronald Reagan and the politics of immigration reform.* Westport, CT: Greenwood Press.

The author argues that the Reagan administration was crippled in its ability to design a sound and effective immigration policy by the lack of accurate and reliable information on this issue and by the president's own ideological hostility toward big government.

270.   Lakachman, R. (1987). *Visions and nightmares: America after Reagan.* New York: Macmillan.

The author speculates upon the shape of American society after Ronald Reagan completes his second term as president and wonders whether any of his Republican successors would approximate his virtuosity in the mobilization of political passion.

271.   Larsen, R. (1994). *Ronald Reagan.* New York: Franklin Watts.

This book charts Reagan's life from his humble beginning in Illinois, to his acting career in Hollywood, to the governorship of California, through his two terms as the 40th president of the United States.

272.   Leamer, L. (1983). *Make-believe: The story of Nancy & Ronald Reagan.* New York: Harper & Row.

This book examines the lives and family of the Reagans, from their courtship, to marriage, to public life.

273.   Lees, J. D., & Turner, M. (Eds.). (1988). *Reagan's first four years: A new beginning?* Manchester, UK: Manchester University Press.

Surveys and analyzes the major political events and the changes that occurred in American national government following Reagan's election.

274.   Lewis, J. (1968). *What makes Reagan run?: A political profile.* New York: McGraw-Hill.

This book tries to explain why California, without widespread poverty or a major state scandal, voted in 1966 to change direction and put Ronald Reagan in the State House in Sacramento as the governor.

275.   Linden, F. van der. (1981). *The real Reagan: What he believes: What he has accomplished: What we can expect from him.* New York: William Morrow.

The author, a White House correspondent and historian, writes about Ronald Reagan, his bid for the American presidency, and his likelihood of reaching the White House.

276.   Lowe, C. (Ed.). (1984). *Reaganomics: The new federalism.* New York: H. W. Wilson.

This book examines the theoretical underpinnings of "Reaganomics" and the new federalism. It traces the history of its implementation during Reagan's first two years in office and focuses on how his economic theories adapted to the political realities.

277.   Maloney, W. E. (1981). *President Ronnie: Dramatic action-packed scenes of President Ronnie's first year in the White House.* New York: Perigee Books.

This is a blend of Reagan's actual movie clips and photographs with satirical attributions to him ranging from his political campaigns to his stint in the White House.

278.   Maranto, R. (1993). *Politics and the bureaucracy in the modern presidency: Careerists and appointees in the Reagan administration.* Westport, CT: Greenwood Press.

The book documents the history of the relationships between careerists and political appointees in the Reagan administration through aggregate data from 118 political appointees and 513 high-level career bureaucrats from 15 federal organizations. The study's findings indicate that the Reagan administration used ideological criteria in personnel policy but on a more modest scale than many have believed.

279.   Marks, S. J. (1996). *If this be treason!* San Marino, CA: Bureau of International Affairs.

Examines how Reagan, Bush, and CIA officials allegedly destroyed the Carter administration in the 1980 presidential election.

280.   Marshall, J., Scott, P. D., & Hunter, J. (1987). *The Iran–Contra connection: Secret teams and covert operations in the Reagan era.* Boston, MA: South End Press.

         This book narrates the circumstances and activities concerning the Iran–Contra affair during the Reagan administration.

281.   Mayer, J., & McManus, D. (1988). *Landslide: The unmaking of the president, 1984-1988.* Boston: Houghton Mifflin.

         Focusing primarily on Reagan's second term in office, this book analyzes his presidency, his alleged indecisive and disengaged demeanor, and an explosive take of the Iran–Contra affair.

282.   McClelland, D. (Ed.). (1983). *Hollywood on Ronald Reagan: Friends and enemies discuss our president, the actor.* Winchester, MA: Faber & Faber.

         Contains exclusive interviews with Hollywood film personalities who have known Ronald Reagan or who simply wish to share their thoughts on the movie star who became the 40th U.S. president.

283.   McClure, A. F., Rice, C. D., & Stewart, W. T. (Eds.). (1988). *Ronald Reagan, his first career: A bibliography of the movie years.* Lewiston, NY: Edwin Mellen Press.

         This book covers Reagan's early years in radio, films, and television and his formative role as president of the Screen Actors Guild.

284.   McFarlane, R. C. (With Zofia Smardz). (1994). *Special trust.* New York: Caddell & Davies.

         The author, former president Reagan's national security adviser, looks back on his life as a great adventure, recounting his experience as a marine officer, a senior official of the State Department, a member of the White House staff for nine years, and his ultimate appointment as national security adviser. Among the major topics that he discusses are the Vietnam War, the failure of Communism in the 1980s, and the Iran–Contra fiasco.

285.   McMahan, J. (1985). *Reagan and the world: Imperial policy in the new Cold War.* New York: Monthly Review Press.

         The author argues that U.S. policy is directed by a quest for global control, military superiority, and economic dominance.

286.   Meese, E., III. (1992). *With Reagan: The inside story.* Washington, D.C.: Regnery Gateway.

The author, who was a former attorney general in the Reagan administration, attempts to provide the reader with an understanding of Ronald Reagan as a political personality, his methods of operation, his qualities as a leader, his philosophy and domestic program, his goals and accomplishments in the realm of foreign affairs, and the net impact of all these matters in terms of national policy and global power.

287.   Meiners, R. E., & Yandle, B. (Eds.). (1989). *Regulation and the Reagan era: Politics, bureaucracy and the public interest.* New York: Holmes & Meier.

In this volume, the contributors look at public debates on reform and the reduction of federal regulatory practice under Ronald Reagan.

288.   Metzger, R. (1989). *Reagan: American icon.* Lewisburg, PA: Bucknell University.

This book documents the rich and varied visions that artists have of the Hollywood actor turned president, Ronald Reagan. It includes a comprehensive chronology, filmography, and televisiongraphy as well as exhaustive visual bibliography that locates reproductions of the Reagan image in books printed during the past 50 years or more.

289.   Moldea, D. E. (1986). *Dark victory: Ronald Reagan, MCA, and the mob.* New York: Viking Press.

This book attempts to illustrates the web of power and manipulation involving the former Music Corporation of America (MCA), Ronald Reagan, former president of the Screen Actors Guild (SAG), and alleged major Mafia figures.

290.   Morley, M. H. (Ed.). (1988). *Crisis and confrontation: Ronald Reagan's foreign policy.* Totowa, NJ: Rowman & Littlefield.

The essays in this volume examine the Reagan administration's foreign policy during the breakdown of détente between the United States and the Soviet Union. It also looks at the growing economic and political conflicts between the United States and its North Atlantic Treaty Organization (NATO) allies and the surge of political and social struggles in the Third World.

291.   Morris, E. (1999). *Dutch: A memoir of Ronald Reagan*. New York: Random House.

Provides a comprehensive biographical narrative of Reagan, from his birth in 1911 in rural Illinois to his varied career: young lifeguard, sportscaster, movie star and union leader, governor, and president.

292.   Morris, J. B. (1995). *The Reagan way*. Minneapolis: Lerner.

This book primarily examines the way some presidents make key decisions, focusing on Reagan's strengths and weaknesses in his major presidential decisions.

293.   Moynihan, D. P. (1988). *Came the revolution: Argument in the Reagan era*. San Diego: Harcourt Brace Jovanovich.

The author, a senior U.S. senator from New York, puts together a sampling of arguments against the policies of the Republican majority and President Ronald Reagan. He takes on "Reaganomics," Star Wars, Iran–Contra affair, and a host of other topics, arguing that the Republican government has failed its mandate to govern.

294.   Muir, W. K., Jr. (1992). *The bully pulpit: The presidential leadership of Ronald Reagan*. San Francisco: ICS Press. (Institute for Contemporary Studies Press).

The author explains the process of Reagan's carefully prepared remarks in public and the purposes that they were intended to serve. Using Reagan's experience, the book sheds light on the means by which people in any walk of life can exercise leadership effectively in a free society.

295.   Nadel, A. (1997). *Flatlining on the field of dreams: Cultural narratives in the films of President Reagan's America*. Piscataway, NJ: Rutgers University Press.

Discusses dozens of films, including *Home Alone, Beettlejuice, Ghost, The Little Mermaid, Working Girl,* and *Who Framed Roger Rabbit?*, and identifies narratives about credit, deregulation, gender, race, and masculinity that defined President Reagan's America.

296.   Niskanen, W. A. (1988). *Reaganomics: An insider's account of the policies and the people*. Washington, D.C.: Cato Institute Press.

The author not only recounts the debates over the Reagan administration's economic program but assesses the program's impact on the federal budget, taxes, regulation, trade, and monetary growth and describes the probable legacy of "Reaganomics."

297.   Noonan, P. (1990). *What I saw at the revolution: A political life in the Reagan era.* New York: Random House.

A former White House speechwriter writes about her experiences, about Ronald Reagan and what his presidency meant, and about what she saw at the "Reagan revolution."

298.   North, O. L. (With William Novak). (1991). *Under fire: An American story.* New York: HapperCollins.

A former National Security Council member narrates his military and political activities as well as his involvement in what became known as the "Iran–Contra" affair, which covers two different secret operations that were carried out by the Reagan administration in the mid-1980s.

299.   Orfield, G. (1994). *Turning back the clock: The Reagan–Bush retreat from civil rights in higher education.* Lanham, MD: University Press of America.

This study reviews policy changes and practices in civil rights enforcement by the Reagan and Bush administrations during the period from 1980 to 1990 and assesses their impact on access to higher education for minorities.

300.   Oye, K. A., Lieber, R. J., & Rothchild, D. (Eds.). (1987). *Eagle resurgent?: The Reagan era in American foreign policy.* Boston: Little, Brown.

This book provides a comprehensive assessment of the wider implications of the first six years of the Reagan administration's foreign policy.

301.   Palmer, J. L. (1986). *Perspectives on the Reagan years.* Washington, D.C.: Urban Institute Press.

The contributors to this book evaluate the record of the Reagan administration by looking at the president's social agenda, his public philosophy, social programs and policies, "Reaganomics," and his White House management style.

302.   Palmer, J. L., & Sawhill, I. V. (Eds.). (1982). *Reagan experiment: An examination of economic and social policies under the Reagan administration.* Washington, D.C.: Urban Institute Press.

This book examines the Reagan administration's economic, budget, tax, and regulatory policies.

303.   Palmer, J. L., & Sawhill, I. V. (Eds.). (1984). *The Reagan record: An assessment of America's changing domestic priorities.* Cambridge, MA: Ballinger.

The contributors to this book document the magnitude and character of the shifts in federal domestic policy as well as some of the policies that President Reagan proposed for consideration. They report on the impact of the changes on people, places, and institutions, and they project probable further impacts.

304.   Payaslian, S. (1996). *U.S. foreign economic and military aid: The Reagan and Bush administrations.* Lanham, MD: University Press of America.

This work explains the extent to which economic, geopolitical, and human rights considerations influenced American foreign aid during the administrations of Reagan and Bush.

305.   Pemberton, W. E. (1997). *Exit with honor: The life and presidency of Ronald Reagan.* Armonk, NY: M. E. Sharpe.

Explores the shaping of Reagan's beliefs and values during his childhood, his leadership of the American conservative movement, and his eminent political career.

306.   Peyer, T., & Seely, H. (1988). *Ronald Reagan's contradictionary of American language.* Boston: Quinlan Press.

This book sheds some light on the words and phrases that Ronald Reagan used throughout his career as governor, candidate, author, and president.

307.   *The public papers of the presidents: Ronald Reagan, 1981–1989.* (1990). Washington, D.C.: U.S. Government Printing Office.

This volume is part of several others that provide both a contemporary reference source and a permanent historical record of the 40th president of the United States.

308.   Quigley, J. (1990). *What does Joan say?: My seven years as White House astrologer to Nancy and Ronald Reagan.* Secaucus, NJ: Birch Lane Press.

The author discusses her astrological work for the Reagans and how she influenced the timing of the president's speeches, public appearances, surgery, and trips, to mention just a few.

309.   Reagan, M. (1989). *First father, first daughter: A memoir*. Boston: Little, Brown.

The author, daughter of President Ronald Reagan, talks about nearly 50 years of daughter–father relationship and about her perceptions of, and involvement in, her father's private and political lives.

310.   Reagan, M. (With Jim Denney). (1997). *The city on a hill: Fulfilling Ronald Reagan's vision for America*. Nashville, TN: Thomas Nelson.

President Reagan's adopted son presents the principles and ideals of his father, what he believes in, what he achieved while in office, and what his vision for America's future is.

311.   Reagan, M. (With Jim Denney). (1998). *The common sense of an uncommon man: The wit, wisdom, and eternal optimism of Ronald Reagan*. Nashville, TN: Thomas Nelson.

The author, Ronald Reagan's son, puts together a collection of his father's public and private words, providing a close-up portrait of America's 40th president. The collection depicts Ronald Reagan in all his many roles— as world leader, conservative icon, orator, actor, and father.

312.   Reagan, M. (With Joe Hyams). (1988). *On the outside looking in*. New York: Zebra Books.

In this book the president's oldest son tells of his life with the Reagan family.

313.   Reagan, N. (With Bill Libby). (1980). *Nancy*. New York: William Morrow.

In this autobiography, the former U.S. first lady tells her own story about her childhood, theater and film career, and life and experiences with Ronald Reagan, the 40th president of the United States.

314.   Reagan, N, (2000). *I love you, Ronnie: The letters of Ronald Reagan to Nancy Reagan*. New York: Random House.

This is a collection of love letters, cards, and telegrams Reagan wrote to his wife, Nancy, over their courtship and marriage.

315.   Reagan, R. (1983). *A time for choosing: The selected speeches of Ronald Reagan, 1961–1982.* Chicago: Regnery Gateway.

Presents Reagan's public rhetoric and delineates the constant theme of his political career—the distinction between freedom and tyranny.

316.   Reagan, R. (1983). *Ronald Reagan talks to America.* Old Greenwich, CT: Devin Adair.

Contains statements and position papers from Reagan's landmark speech on behalf of Barry Goldwater on October 27, 1964, to his subsequent political career.

317.   Reagan, R. (1989). *Speaking my mind: Selected speeches.* New York: Simon & Schuster.

This collection of speeches from Reagan's White House years provides insight into who he is, where he came from, what he believes in, and what he tried to do as a result. The book contains verbatim transcripts with no deletions for misstatements that he may have made or for hopes that he voiced that never came true.

318.   Reagan, R. (1990). *An American life: The autobiography.* New York: Simon & Schuster.

This book provides a self-portrait of Reagan's life—private and public—and tells us with all the uncompromising candor his early years and extraordinary career as president of the United States.

319.   Reagan, R. (With Richard G. Hubler). (1965). *Where's the rest of me?* New York: Duell, Sloan & Pearce.

In this autobiography, Reagan candidly narrates his life history and explains why he decided to find the rest of himself after his career as an actor.

320.   Regan, D. T. (1988). *For the record: From Wall Street to Washington.* San Diego: Harcourt Brace Jovanovich.

This book is the memoir of the author after more than six years of public service as the secretary of treasury and as chief of staff in the White House under Ronald Reagan. The author attempts to describe the president whom he served, the people whom he encountered in the course of that service, and the events in which he participated, exactly as he remembered.

321. Rimmerman, C. A. (1993). *Presidency by plebiscite: The Reagan–Bush era in institutional perspective.* Boulder, CO: Westview Press.

Using the Reagan and Bush presidencies as comparative case studies, this book details the changing manifestation of presidential power in the late twentieth century.

322. Ritter, K., & Henry, D. (1992). *Ronald Reagan: The great communicator.* New York: Greenwood Press.

This book is the study of President Ronald Reagan's oratory, providing a record of his responses to several decades of American political life.

323. Rogin, M. P. (1987). *Ronald Reagan, the movie and other episodes in political demonology.* Berkeley: University of California Press.

The book examines why and how fear of the subversive has governed American politics, from the racial conflicts of the early republic to the Hollywood anti-Communism of Ronald Reagan.

324 Ronald Reagan Presidential Foundation. (2001). *Ronald Reagan: An American hero: His voice, his value, his vision.* London: Dorling Kindersley. Using more than 500 photographs and brief essays, this book chronicles the achievements of America's 40th president.

325. Ronald Reagan Presidential Foundation. (1998). *A shining city: The legacy of Ronald Reagan.* New York: Simon & Schuster.

Laced with 45 color photos, this book contains powerful passages from Ronald Reagan's best postpresidential speeches, with tributes from leaders and important personalities from around the world.

326. Ryan, F. J., Jr. (Ed.). (1995). *Ronald Reagan: The wisdom and humor of the great communicator.* San Francisco: Collins.

This is a unique collection of words and photographs about former U.S. president Ronald Reagan, who is affectionately dubbed the "Great Communicator."

327. Salamon, L. M., & Lund, M. S. (Eds.). (1984). *The Reagan presidency and the governing of America.* Washington, D.C.: Urban Institute Press.

One of six collections of analyses by leading scholars examining the effects of the Reagan administration on America's politics and its governing institutions and processes.

328.   Sahu, A. P., & Tracy, R. L. (Eds). (1991). *The economic legacy of the Reagan years: Euphoria or chaos?* New York: Praeger.

         This is a wide-ranging collection of essays written by respected economists analyzing the empirical evidence of the Reagan presidency. By detailing the administration's legacy, which includes low employment and economic growth, and its negative effects, such as unprecedented deficits and regulatory chaos, the book provides some tentative conclusions as to whether the Reagan years produced an economic miracle or paved the way for economic disaster.

329.   Schaller, M. (1992). *Reckoning with Reagan: America and its president in the 1980s.* New York: Oxford University Press.

         The book provides insight into the Reagan years, weighing the president's great personal and political popularity against the effects of his economic, social, diplomatic, and strategic decisions.

330.   Scheer, R. (1982). *With enough shovels: Reagan, Bush and nuclear war.* New York: Random House.

         This book treats Ronald Reagan's plan for waging and winning a nuclear war with the Soviet Union and his obsession with a strategy of confrontation.

331.   Schieffer, B., & Gates, G. P. (1989). *The acting president: Ronald Reagan and the supporting players who helped him create the illusion that held America spellbound.* New York: E. P. Dutton.

         Drawing on hundreds of newspapers and magazines, the authors dig deep into how decisions were made and how events unfolded during the Reagan administration.

332.   Schmertz, E. J., Datlof, N., & Ugrinsky, A. (Eds.) (1997). *President Reagan and the world.* Westport, CT: Greenwood Press.

         Prepared under the auspices of Hofstra University in New York, this book explores the Reagan administration's interaction with the world community and provides a survey of the important global issues that arose during that administration.

333.   Schmertz, E. J., Datlof, N., & Ugrinsky, A. (Eds.) (1997). *Ronald Reagan's America. Vols. 1 and 2.* Westport, CT: Greenwood Press.

This two-volume book, based on a conference held at Hofstra University in New York, provides a comprehensive exploration and exposition of Reagan policies and the essential details that make up those policies.

334.   Schorr, A. L. (1988). *Common decency: Domestic policies after Reagan.* New Haven, CT: Yale University Press.

Critiques America's social policies under the Reagan administration and offers proposals for improving income distribution, housing, health, and education.

335.   Schulman, S. (1994). *My American history: Lesbian and gay life during the Reagan/Bush years.* New York: Routledge.

This is a collection of essays by the author (written over an 11-year period) covering such issues as the inauguration of Ronald Reagan, the rise of the political Right, the attacks on abortion, the sex wars in the feminist movement, the AIDS pandemic, and the new lesbian activism.

336.   Schwab, L. M. (1991). *The illusion of a conservative Reagan revolution.* New Brunswick, NJ: Transaction.

This book argues that policy developments during the 1980s and the Reagan era were not fundamentally conservative.

337.   Schweizer, P. (1994). *Victory: The Reagan administration's secret strategy that hastened the collapse of the Soviet Union.* New York: Atlantic Monthly Press.

Based on exclusive interviews with key Reagan administration staffers, the author provides details of how the administration undermined the Soviet economy and its dwindling resource base and subverted the Kremlin's hold on its global empire.

338.   Scofield, E. (1983). *Reagan, "B" actor, "A" president?* Hollywood, CA: American Progress Enterprises.

This book tries to elucidate the problems, both domestic and foreign, that arose during the Reagan administration. It ferrets out the causes and suggests why they arose and how to reverse the process.

339.   Scott, J. M. (1996). *Deciding to intervene: The Reagan doctrine and American foreign policy.* Durham, NC: Duke University Press.

This book uses a comparative case study method to examine the historical, intellectual, and ideological origins of the Reagan doctrine as it was applied to Afghanistan, Angola, Cambodia, Nicaragua, Mozambique, and Ethiopia.

340.   Shanley, R. A. (1992). *Presidential influence and environmental policy.* Westport, CT: Greenwood Press.

This book examines the Reagan administrative presidency strategy and its impact on environmentally related policies throughout the Reagan years and assesses its legacy for the Bush administration.

341.   Short, C. B. (1989). *Ronald Reagan and the public lands: America's conservation debate, 1979–1984.* College Station: Texas A&M University Press.

This is a study of public lands policy during the Reagan administration.

342.   Shull, S. A. (1993). *A kinder, gentler racism?: The Reagan–Bush civil rights legacy.* Armonk, NY: M. E. Sharpe.

This volume compares Ronald Reagan and George Bush with other recent presidents, including Bill Clinton, to show how presidents can influence the policy-making process.

343.   Sick, G. (1991). *October surprise: America's hostages in Iran and the election of Ronald Reagan.* New York: Times Books.

The book brings to light new information and allegations about how the 1980 Reagan–Bush presidential campaign cut a deal with Iran to delay the release of 52 Americans held hostage in Tehran. It argues that this deal not only prevented then-president Jimmy Carter from reaping the political benefits of an early hostage release but also hobbled his ability to exercise the full powers of his elective office.

344.   Skinner, K. K., Anderson, A., & Anderson, M. (Eds.) (2001). *Reagan in his own hand: The writings of Ronald Reagan that reveal his revolutionary vision for America.* New York: Free Press.

This book contains the original writings of the pre-presidential era of Ronald Reagan. It presents Reagan's vision and philosophy on public policy issues through his radio writings, speeches, letters, short fiction, poetry, sports stories, and newspaper articles.

345.   Skinner, K. K., Anderson, M., & Anderson, A. (Eds.) (2001). *Stories in his own hand: The everyday wisdom of Ronald Reagan*. New York: Free Press.

         This book focuses on Reagan's storytelling abilities used mostly to inspire, uplift, and to emphasize to his listeners the true meaning of life generally.

346.   Skoug, K. N., Jr. (1996). *The United States and Cuba under Reagan and Shultz*. Westport, CT: Greenwood Press.

         This book focuses on U.S. diplomatic relations, describing six years of conflict management, involving much confrontation and selective diplomacy, during which Cuba was put progressively on the defense by political, economic, and military actions.

347.   Sloan, I. J. (Ed.). (1990). *Ronald W. Reagan 1911—Chronology-documents bibliographical aids*. Dobbs Ferry, NY: Oceana..

         This is a record of events and accomplishments regarding the political life of Ronald Reagan from his tenure as California governor to his White House years.

348.   Sloan, J. W. (1999). *The Reagan effect: Economics and presidential leadership*. Lawrence: University Press of Kansas.

         The book attempts to evaluate debates between conservatives and liberals concerning Reagan's economic policies and legacy.

349.   Slosser, B. (1984). *Reagan inside out*. Waco, TX: Word Books.

         Examines Reagan's efforts to provide leadership to America, and analyzes how he thought and how his beliefs might bring any meaningful change to America.

350.   Smith, C. (1996). *Resisting Reagan: The U.S. Central America peace movement*. Chicago: University of Chicago Press.

         This is a comprehensive study of this peace movement, focusing on three most important campaigns, notably, Witness for Peace, Sanctuary, and the Pledge Resistance. It demonstrates the centrality of morality as a political behavior, highlights the importance of political opportunities in movement outcomes, and examines the social structuring of insurgent consciousness.

351.   Smith, G. H. (1968). *Who is Ronald Reagan?* New York: Pyramid Books.

This book examines Reagan's political career, focusing on the probability that he might join the race for the American presidency and what his chances are for winning the White House.

352.   Smith, H. (1988). *The power game: How Washington works.* New York: Random House.

Drawing heavily on the Reagan period, this book looks at what works well in the political power game.

353.   Smith, H., Burt, R., Silk, L., & Lindsey, R. (1980). *Reagan: The man, the president.* New York: Macmillan.

The authors trace the rise of Ronald Reagan to power from the day that he sat on the national political stage on October 27, 1964, when he made a half-hour televised speech for the Republican presidential candidate, Barry Goldwater, to his election as the 40th president of the United States.

354.   Smith, S. K., & Wertman, D. A. (1992). *US–West European relations during the Reagan Years: The perspective of West European publics.* New York: St. Martin's Press.

Using extensive survey data, the authors examine the major issues that dominated U.S.–West European relations during the Reagan years. These include security issues, terrorism, economic relations, and superpower relations.

355.   Smith, T. B. (With Carter Henderson). (1992). *White House doctor.* Lanham, MD: Madison Books.

The physician to President Ronald Reagan chronicles medical events during his tenure at the White House.

356.   Smith, V. K. (Ed.). (1984). *Environmental policy under Reagan's executive order: The role of benefit-cost analysis.* Chapel Hill: University of North Carolina Press.

The essays in this book assess the impact on environmental policy of Executive Order No. 12291, issued by Reagan, which required a benefit-cost analysis for all major new regulations.

357.   Smith, W. F. (1991). *Law and justice in the Reagan administration: Memoirs of an Attorney General.* Stanford, CA: Hoover Institute Press.

The author, who served as Ronald Reagan's first attorney general, details his views and experiences in the administration.

358.	Snyder, W. P., & Brown, J. (Eds.). (1988). *Defense policy in the Reagan administration*. Washington, D.C.: National Defense University Press.

This book examines the policies and programs that were the center of controversy during the Reagan years, concentrating on the most important issues like Strategic Defense Initiative (SDI), the 600-ship navy, and the hefty increase in the American defense budget.

359.	Souza, P. (1992). *Unguarded moments: Behind-the-scenes photographs of President Ronald Reagan*. Forth Worth, TX: Summit Group.

A collection of photographs and text depicting not only history in the making but also the personal side of Ronald Reagan.

360.	Spada, J. (2001). *Ronald Reagan: His life in pictures*. New York: St. Martin's Press.

This book contains more than 350 photographs depicting the extraordinary life story of America's 40th president, Ronald Reagan.

361.	Speaks, L. (With Robert Pack). (1988). *Speaking out: The Reagan presidency from inside the White House*. New York: Scribner.

The former White House spokesman provides his personal account of his six-year service (from 1981 to 1987) of what went on in the Reagan White House and what his role was in those events.

362.	Stockman, D. A. (1986). *The triumph of politics: Why the Reagan revolution failed*. New York: Harper & Row.

The author, a former official of the Reagan administration, tells the story of the "Reagan revolution," arguing that it made so little difference to the administration's poverty program.

363.	Strober, D. H., & Strober, G. S. (1998). *Reagan: The man and his presidency*. Boston: Houghton Mifflin.

This book contains interviews of more than 100 key players of the Reagan years as well as the major news stories of the American 1980s, all of them giving a composite portrait of the presidency of Ronald Reagan and chronicling national and international politics of the period.

364.   Strock, J. M. (1998). *Reagan on leadership: Executive lessons from the Great Communicator.* Rocklin, CA: Prima.

This book provides important information for understanding President Ronald Reagan's leadership and management styles, as well as his communication skills and practices.

365.   Stuckey, M. E. (1989). *Getting into the game: The pre-presidential rhetoric of Ronald Reagan.* New York: Praeger.

The book examines politics as practiced by Reagan through the analysis of his rhetoric from his years as the California state governor to his campaign for the presidency in 1980.

366.   Stuckey, M. E. (1990). *Playing the game: The presidential rhetoric of Ronald Reagan.* New York: Praeger.

The author explores the rhetoric of the "Reagan Revolution," emphasizing how the rhetoric supported, impeded, and affected his policy goals and political success.

367.   Sullivan, G. (1985). *Ronald Reagan.* Englewood Cliffs, NJ: Julian Messner.

This is a detailed study of the life of the 40th president of the United States, Ronald Reagan, chronicling his early childhood, film career, and his years in state and national politics.

368.   Talbott, S. (1984). *The Russians and Reagan.* New York: Vantage Books.

Examines the Reagan administration's attitude toward the Soviet Union and traces the steps that have led the leaders of that country to feel that it is impossible for them to deal with the Reagan administration.

369.   Thompson, K. W. (Ed.). (1983). *The White House on the presidency: News management and co-option.* Lanham, MD: University Press of America.

This volume offers the opinions of three leading senior White House journalists—James Deakin, Helen Thomas, and Frank Cormier—regarding the relationship between the president and the press. They agree that the White House reporters must pursue the truth wherever it may lead them.

370.   Thompson, K. W. (Ed.). (1992). *Leadership in the Reagan presidency: Seven intimate perspectives.* Lanham, MD: Madison Books.

This book draws on a broadly representative group of interpreters whose histories shed light on the different facets of the Reagan administration.

371. Thompson, K. W. (Ed.). (1992). *The Reagan to Bush experience, Vol. 8.* Lanham, MD: University Press of America.

This volume evaluates the presidential transition from Ronald Reagan to George Bush.

372. Thompson, K. W. (Ed.). (1993). *Foreign policy in the Reagan presidency: Nine intimate perspectives.* Lanham, MD: University Press of America.

This volume provides differing viewpoints about the foreign policy directions in the Reagan administration

373. Thompson, K. W. (Ed.). (1993). *Leadership in the Reagan presidency Part II: Eleven intimate perspectives.* Lanham, MD: University Press of America.

In this volume, leading political figures who worked closely with President Ronald Reagan examine him as a leader.

374. Thompson, K. W. (Ed.). (1997). *The Reagan presidency: Ten intimate perspectives of Ronald Reagan.* Lanham, MD: University Press of America.

This volume examines the political forces and personal characteristics that shaped the Reagan presidency. In particular, it addresses the essential themes of his presidency—notably, governance, the role of communication, domestic policy, international trade, international policy, and post–Cold War strategy.

375. Trimble, V. H. (1980). *Reagan: The man from Main Street.* Cincinnati: Mosaic Press.

This book provides the life story of Ronald Reagan up to the time he was elected president of the United States.

376. Valis, W. (Ed.). (1981). *The future under President Reagan.* Westport, CT: Arlington House.

This book examines various aspects of Reagan's personal life, character and personality, his career, and the policies and programs that he was expected to propose and support.

377. Vaughn, S. (1994). *Ronald Reagan in Hollywood: Movies and politics.* Cambridge, UK: Cambridge University Press.

Explores the relationship between the motion picture industry and American politics through the prism of Reagan's film career at Warner Brothers.

378. Walsh, K. T. (1997). *Ronald Reagan.* New York: Park Lane Press.

Based primarily on exclusive interviews and access to major figures of the Reagan era, the book shows us what drove Ronald Reagan from a small flat in Tampico, Illinois, to the White House and what obstacles he overcame to get there.

379. Wead, D., & Wead, B. (1980). *Reagan, in pursuit of the presidency— 1980.* Plainfield, NJ: Haven Books.

This small-sized book examines the former American movie star and governor of California Ronald Reagan's political campaign for the 1980 U.S. presidential election. Specifically, it looks at his politics and his faith, as well as his position on inflation, taxation, recession, abortion, strengthening America's international image, and the need for spiritual renewal.

380. Weiler, M., & Pierce, W. B. (Eds.). (1992). *Reagan and public discourse in America.* Tuscaloosa: University of Alabama Press.

The essays in this book assess the rhetorical legacy of the Reagan presidency, focusing on a variety of domestic and foreign policy controversies and identifying a broad range of persuasive strategies and devices to reveal how Reagan both appropriated and transformed American public discourse in the 1980s.

381. Weintraub, S., & Goodstein, M. (Eds.). (1983). *Reaganomics in the stagflation economy.* Philadelphia: University of Pennsylvania Press.

Contains papers presented at the Third Annual Sewanee Economics Symposium on October 1–3, 1981, which discussed the federal budget debate about stagflation under President Ronald Reagan's exercise in fiscal fitness.

382. White, F. C., & Gill, W. J. (1981). *Why Reagan won: A narrative history of the conservative movement 1964–1981.* Chicago: Regnery Gateway.

The book is about Ronald Reagan's political career and the conservative movement that he so ably and so courageously represents.

383.   White, J. K. (1988). *The new politics of old values*. Hanover, NH: University of New England Press.

Using Ronald Reagan's presidency as a case study, this book examines how widely shared values can be utilized to garner public support and move a nation forward.

384.   Wiarda, H. J. (1994). *American foreign policy towards Latin America in the 80s and 90s: Issues and controversies from Reagan to Bush*. New York: New York University Press.

This book examines the fundamental tenets and ideology behind the United States' policy toward Latin America during the Reagan–Bush era.

385.   Williamson, R. S. (1990). *Reagan's federalism: His efforts to decentralize government*. Lanham, MD: University Press of America.

This book reveals the inside story of how President Ronald Reagan sought to take power and authority from the federal government and the Washington establishment and return it to state and local governments.

386.   Wills, G. (1987). *Reagan's America: Innocents at home*. Garden City, NY: Doubleday.

The book looks at how President Ronald Reagan became an icon and an embodiment of all that Americans believed about themselves—that they are optimistic individualists, tough yet God fearing, and blessed with special destiny.

387.   Wink, J. (1996). *On the brink: The dramatic, behind-the-scenes saga of the Reagan era and the men and women who won the Cold War*. New York: Simon & Schuster.

This book examines America's Cold War victory in the Reagan era. It is told as narrative, largely through the eyes of the key players on various sides, from their rise in the late 1970s through the 1980s, to the conflict's denouement.

388.   Wirls, D. (1991). *Buildup: The politics of defense in the Reagan era*. Ithaca, NY: Cornell University Press.

The author examines the military buildup of the Reagan administration, focusing on the Strategic Defense Initiative (SDI), the nuclear weapons peace movement, and the military reform movement.

389.   Wofsy, L. (1990). *Before the point of no return: An exchange of views on the Cold War, the Reagan doctrine, and what is to come.* New York: Monthly Review Press.

This is a collection of essays and letters about the Cold War and possible reasons for the escalation of the arms race and increased hostility between the United States and the former Soviet Union.

390.   Wymbs, N. E. (1987). *A place to go back to: Ronald Reagan in Dixon, Illinois.* New York: Vantage Press.

This book contains information of a personal nature on the Reagan family, especially about the early molding of Ronald Reagan, America's 40th president.

391.   Wymbs, N. E., & Gee, C. G. (1996). *Ronald Reagan's crusade.* Ft. Lauderdale, FL: VYTIS Publishing Co.

This is a biography of Reagan's boyhood days in Dixon, Illinois. It explores the many differing perceptions of him, from his popularity as a movie star in Hollywood to his early and deep love of country, and his strong sense of patriotism.

392.   Yarbrough, T. E. (Ed.). (1985). *The Reagan administration and human rights.* New York: Praeger.

This book contains 10 original essays that examine the influence of the Reagan administration on the Justice Department, voting rights, gender discrimination, the Equal Rights Amendment (ERA), education, housing discrimination, the "pro-family" agenda, affirmative action, the Civil Rights Commission, and international human rights policy.

393.   Zucker, I., & David, M. (1976). *Ronnie runs wild.* Los Angeles: Mark David.

Contains pictures of Ronald Reagan as depicted in several of his movies with attributable satirical quotations.

GEORGE BUSH

394.   Baker, J. A., III. (With Thomas M. Defrank). (1995). *The politics of diplomacy: Revolution, war and peace, 1989–1992.* New York: G. P. Putnam.

The former U.S. secretary of state in the Bush administration recounts his political experience during the 48 months that he served in that position.

395.   Barilleaux, R. J., & Stuckey, M. E. (Eds.). (1992). *Leadership and the Bush presidency: Prudence or drift in an era of change?* Westport, CT: Greenwood Press.

The chapters in this volume offer a comprehensive look at the Bush presidency and Bush's legacy for future presidents.

396.   Beschloss, M. R., & Talbot, S. (1993). *At the highest levels: The inside story of the end of the Cold War.* Boston: Little, Brown.

The authors examine U.S.–Soviet relationship, arguing that the highly personal way in which George Bush and Mikhail Gorbachev closely attuned to each other eventually caused both leaders to lose touch with their domestic constituencies.

397.   Blanton, T. (Ed.). (1995). *White House E-mail: The top secret computer messages the Reagan/Bush White House tried to destroy.* New York: New Press.

This book contains the highest-level White House E-mail communications on the most secret national security affairs of the United States during the 1980s.

398.   Blanton, T., & Kirp, D. (With Barry Bluestone). (1995). *Eyes on the president: George Bush: History in essays and cartoons.* Occidental, CA: Chronos.

This is a collection of essays and political cartoons reprinted from the national press, chronicling national and international events and issues that characterized the Bush presidency.

399.   Buchman, D. D. (1989). *Our 41st president George Bush.* New York: Scholastic.

This small book looks at the life and career of George Bush, America's 41st president.

400.   Bush, B. (1994). *Barbara Bush: A memoir.* New York: Scribner.

Relying on diaries, tapes, letters, and personal memory, former American first lady Barbara Bush recounts her early years and public life at the side of her husband, George Bush, 41st president of the United States.

401.   Bush, G. (1999). *All the best, George Bush: My life in letters and other writings*. New York: Scribner.

In this book, which contains a collection of letters, diary entries, and memos, former president George Bush shares his private thoughts in his correspondence throughout his life, from his teenage years to the postpresidency.

402.   Bush, G. (With Victor Gold). (1987). *Looking forward*. Garden City, NY: Doubleday.

In this book, American vice president George Bush shares his life story, personal philosophy, goals, and hopes for the future.

403.   Bush, G. (With Doug Wead). (1988). *Man of integrity*. Eugene, OR: Harvest House.

This interview-based book tells of the life and times of George Bush, especially about his World War II days, and focuses on his stance on several issues, including abortion, AIDS, balanced budget, capital punishment, Central America, equal rights, religious freedom, South Africa, space policy, and tax reform.

404.   Bush, G., & Scowcroft, B. (1998). *A world transformed*. New York: Alfred A. Knopf.

This book focuses on the years 1989 to 1991 during Bush's term, when such critical world events as the massacre at Tiananmen Square, the fall of the Berlin Wall, the disintegration of the former Soviet Union, and the Persian Gulf War occurred. Assisted by his former national security adviser, Brent Scowcroft, Bush provides a vivid narrative of how these crises were dealt with at the highest level.

405.   Campbell, C., & Rockman, B. A. (Eds.). (1991). *The Bush presidency: First appraisals*. Chatham, NJ: Chatham House.

The contributors to this volume primarily assess how George Bush was doing in the White House. They describe events and judge how he is handling them.

406.   Congressional Quarterly (CQ). (1989). *President Bush: The challenge ahead*. Washington, D.C.: Author.

Part of the Congressional Quarterly series that examine the Bush administration's policies, activities, and programs and highlights his speeches to Congress and presidential Inaugural Address.

407.   *The cumulated indexes to the public papers of the president of the United States: George Bush, 1989–1992*. (1995). Lanham, MD: Bernan Press.

These cumulated indexes provide essential information on the presidency of George Bush, documenting his administration's policies, actions, and decisions.

408.   Davis, S. M. (1989). *The Bush presidency and South Africa: Congress and the sanctions outlook*. Braamfontein, SA: South African Institute of International Affairs.

This booklet asserts that the inauguration of George Bush as the U.S. president marked a new acceptance in Washington of sanctions as a legitimate and necessary tool of American foreign policy toward South Africa.

409.   Drummy, J. J. (1991). *The establishment's man*. Appleton, WI: Western Islands.

Examines the record of George Bush as has been assessed by an array of commentators from both conservative and liberal points of the political spectrum.

410.   Fitzwater, M. (1995). *Call the briefing: Bush and Reagan, Sam and Helen—A decade with presidents and the press*. New York: Times Books.

The author, who was the former White House press secretary in the administrations of both Reagan and Bush, throws light on the few major events between 1983 and 1993 that show the blend of personalities in the White House, how they influenced national life, how the media fitted in, and the fragility of his own life as a spokesperson.

411.   Goodgame, D. (1992). *Marching in place: The status quo presidency of George Bush*. New York: Simon & Schuster.

Provides a critical account of President Bush's leadership style and his handling of domestic and foreign policies.

412.   Graubard, S. R. (1992). *Mr. Bush's war: Adventures in the politics of illusion*. New York: Hill & Wang.

The author attacks Bush's motive for launching the Persian Gulf War in early 1991, arguing that it was a great failure because it resolved nothing and settled nothing.

413. Green, F. (1989). *George Bush: An intimate portrait.* New York: Hippocrene Books.

This book provides an intimate look at the life of George Bush, focusing primarily on his early years and how his adult character was shaped by family experience and world realities.

414. Greene, J. R. (2000). *The presidency of George Bush.* Lawrence: University Press of Kansas.

This book uses the entire range of literature on the 41st president—including the Bush Papers at the George Bush Presidential Library at Texas A&M University—and draws on key interviews with members of his administration and with Bush himself to paint a comprehensive history of his administration.

415. Haas, L. J. (1990). *Running on empty: Bush, Congress, and the politics of bankrupt government.* Homewood, IL: Business One Irwin.

This book focuses on the politics of solving the deficit problem during the Bush administration.

416. Heagerty, L. E. (Ed.). (1993). *Eyes on the president: George Bush: History in essays and cartoons.* Occidental, CA: Chronos.

The book offers an appraisal of the Bush presidency in essays and 210 political cartoons that help the reader to understand the issues and events of his administration.

417. Hendra, T. (1992). *Born to run things: An utterly unauthorized biography of George Bush.* New York: Villard Books.

Fully illustrated, this book takes a satirical look at George Bush, the man and his presidency.

418. Hill, D. M., & Williams, P. (Eds.). (1994). *The Bush presidency: Triumphs and adversities.* New York: St. Martin's Press.

The essays in this book cover the momentous four years of the Bush presidency and how his leadership impacted American and world history.

419.   Hyams, J. (1991). *Flight of the avenger: George Bush at war.* San Diego: Harcourt Brace Jovanovich.

This book particularly tells of President Bush's days as a torpedo bomber pilot over the Pacific during World War II and his dramatic rescue after he and his squadron buddies were shot down in a Japanese artillery assault.

420.   Hybel, A. R. (1993). *Power over rationality: The Bush administration and the Gulf crisis.* Albany: State University of New York Press.

The book proposes a typology of decision-making aptitudes designed to explain foreign policy decisions and to assess the quality of the process, using the Persian Gulf War as a case study.

421.   Ide, A. F. (1989). *Bush–Quayle: The Reagan legacy.* Irving, TX: Scholars Books.

In this book the author defined the parameters of the future Bush–Quayle administration and how it was expected to affect the lives of millions of the poor, the homeless, and minorities, as well as its far reaching role in the realities of the dwindling middle class.

422.   Kolb, C. (1994). *White House daze: The unmaking of domestic policy in the Bush years.* New York: Free Press.

This book presents a picture of the inner workings of the Bush White House.

423.   Levy, P. B. (1996). *Encyclopedia of the Reagan–Bush years.* Westport, CT: Greenwood Press.

This volume provides information on the key developments and figures of the Reagan–Bush years, 1980–1992. The book features over 250 entries on key personalities, issues, events, political and governmental developments, foreign and domestic concerns, laws, terms and catchphrases, and social and cultural trends of the era.

424.   Mervin, D. (1998). *George Bush and the guardianship presidency.* New York: Macmillan.

Using extensive interviews with White House staff, the author provides a provocative analysis of the Bush presidency, focusing on the strengths and weaknesses in his approach to presidential leadership. This book not only casts light on Bush's record in office but also helps to resolve methodological problems that arise in the study of the presidency generally.

425.   Millet, L. (2000). *George Bush, dark prince of love: A presidential romance.* New York: Scribner.

This is a political satire of the Bush presidency.

426.   Parmet, H. S. (1997). *George Bush: The life of a Lone Star Yankee.* New York: Scribner.

Using documentary material and personal interviews with President Bush, the author shapes the biography and character of the 41st president of the United States.

427.   Pemberton, W. E. (1993). *George Bush.* Vero Beach, FL: Rourke.

This book provides a biography of Bush, emphasizing his background and life in politics.

428.   Podhoretz, J. (1993). *Hell of a ride: Backstage at the White House follies, 1989–1993.* New York: Simon & Schuster.

Chronicles the decline and fall of George Bush through the eyes of people who worked in his White House.

429.   Powell, C. L. (1995). *My American journey.* New York: Random House.

One of America's most prominent public figures writes about his life and about his experiences as the twelfth chairman of the Joint Chiefs of Staff under Presidents George Bush and Bill Clinton.

430.   *The public papers of the presidents of the United States, 1992-93: George Bush.* (1993). 2 Vols. Washington, D.C.: U.S. Government Printing Office.

This book contains the papers and speeches of the 41st president of the United States that were issued by the Office of Press Secretary during the period August 1, 1992, to January 20, 1993.

431.   Rozell, M. J. (1996). *The press and the Bush presidency. Westport, CT: Greenwood Press.*

In this book the author reviews press coverage of the Bush presidency and offers a comparative analysis of the relations between modern presidents and the press.

432. Sadofsky, D. (1993). *The question of privacy in public policy: An analysis of the Reagan–Bush era*. Westport, CT: Greenwood Press.

This study examines the role of privacy in American political thought, with special emphasis on the rise, implementation, and consequences of the conservative social policies of the Reagan–Bush era as they relate to the question of privacy.

433. Sandak, C. R. (1991). *The Bushes*. New York: Crestwood House.

This book provides an account of the life of George Bush and his family, emphasizing on his years as America's 41st president.

434. Sargent, J. F., Jr. (Ed.). (1989). *President Bush's point of view*. Washington, D.C.: Braddock Communications.

This book contains quotations selected from George Bush's 1988 presidential campaign that reflect his core beliefs and the direction that he wants to take America.

435. Stefoff, R. (1991). *George H. W. Bush: 41st president of the United States*. Ada, OK: Garrett Educational Corp.

This book examines the life of George Bush, including his World War II days, work in Texas oil fields, first years in the White House, and the war in the Persian Gulf.

436. Stinnett, R. B. (1991). *George Bush: His World War II years*. Missoula, MT: Pictorial Histories.

Chronicles former President George Bush's years as a naval aviator during World War II.

437. Sullivan, G. (1989). *George Bush*. Englewood Cliffs, NJ: Julian Messner.

Filled with pictures, this biography provides vital statistics about the man who became America's 41st president.

438. Tarpley, W. G., & Chaitkin, A. (1992). *George Bush: The unauthorized biography*. Washington, D.C.: Executive Intelligence Review.

Traces the private and public lives of Bush and provides insight into the private forces dominating both Republican and Democratic Parties—and the man who occupied the highest seat of power in the nation.

439.   Thompson, K. W. (Ed.). (1997). *The Bush presidency: Ten intimate perspectives of George Bush*. Lanham, MD: University Press of America.

This volume examines the essential topics that surrounded the Bush presidency—notably, leadership, governance, personal selection, foreign policy, and the 1992 presidential election.

440.   Thompson, K. W. (Ed.). (1998). *The Bush presidency—Part II: Ten intimate perspectives of George Bush*. Lanham, MD: University Press of America.

People who worked with President Bush provide insight into his actions as a communicator, his performance as a domestic and international president, and particularly his search for a grand strategy in foreign policy, through his dealings with Russia, China, and NAFTA.

441.   Tiefer, C. (1994). *The semi-sovereign presidency: The Bush administration's strategy for governing without Congress*. Boulder, CO: Westview Press.

This book is the first analysis of the Bush presidency's strategy regarding separation of powers—the constitutional relationship of the president and Congress.

442.   Valdez, D. (1997). *George Herbert Walker Bush: A photographic profile*. College Station: Texas A&M University Press.

In colorful and dramatic detail, this book chronicles the life and career of America's 41st president, from his childhood, to his military service, to his stint in the White House.

443.   Wiese, A. E. (1979). *George Bush*. Washington, D.C.: Political Profiles.

In this booklet, Bush talks in two interview pieces about the American economy, inflation, energy, Richard Nixon, and major issues of national and international importance.

444.   Woodward, B. (1991). *The commanders*. New York: Simon & Schuster.

Provides a portrait of the men behind the 1991 Persian Gulf War, noting that President George Bush was the key decision maker behind it all.

445.   Woodward, B. (1999). *Shadow: Five presidents and the legacy of Watergate*. New York: Simon & Schuster.

This book examines how Presidents Ford, Carter, Reagan, Bush, and Clinton struggled to cope with and adapt to the multiple legacies of Watergate.

Addendum

At the time of going to press, ex-president Jimmy Carter has released his latest book titled *Christmas in Plains*, bringing the total number of annotated works in this book to 446.

446.   Carter, J. (2001). *Christmas in Plains*. New York: Simon & Schuster.

In this book America's 39th president reminiscents about how Christmas celebrations in his native Plains, Georgia, meant to him, his family, and friends.

Author Index

*References in **bold-face** type indicate entry numbers in bibliographic section only. References in* roman *indicate page numbers in the text.*

Subject Index

Reference numbers indicate page numbers.

About the Author

CLEMENT E. ASANTE is an independent scholar and consultant specializing in the media, program evaluation, and grant proposal writing. Currently President of ClemBet Group, a nonprofit agency committed to improving lifestyles of the disadvantaged, he is also founder and Executive Director of African Media Research and Development, an international organization geared toward improving the quality of journalism education and training in Africa.